THE ESSENTIAL
MANIFESTING
GUIDEBOOK

THE ESSENTIAL
MANIFESTING
GUIDEBOOK

Simple Steps To Create
The Life You Truly Desire

TRISH MCKINNLEY

7th STAR
PUBLISHING

DAYTON, OH

Trish McKinnley/7th Star Publishing
251 W. Central Ave., Suite 140, Springboro, Ohio / USA 45066-9998

Ordering Information:
Quantity sales. Special discounts are available on quantity purchases by corporations, associations, and others. For details, contact the "Special Sales Department" at the address above.

The Essential Manifesting Guidebook / Trish McKinnley. —1st ed.
ISBN 979-8-9893162-3-6

To all the dreamers, seekers, and believers,

This book is lovingly dedicated to you.

May the pages within be a gentle reminder that you
are the architect of your own destiny, capable of
manifesting the most beautiful life imaginable.

As you embark on this journey of cosmic exploration and self-
discovery, may you feel the warmth of the universe embracing
you, guiding you, and celebrating your infinite potential.

In your hands lies the power to manifest a life filled with love,
prosperity, and joy. Know that you are cherished, and your dreams
are worth pursuing. With each turn of the page, may you sense the
love and encouragement that went into crafting these words, as
you embark on a path of transformation, joy, and manifestation.

This book is a testament to the belief that your desires are
valid, and your future is bright. May you manifest with love,
purpose, and unwavering faith in your own magic.

With boundless love and blessings,

Love,

Trish

CONTENTS

1   *Welcome*

5   *Manifesting 101*

7   *How to Use This Book*

SECTION 1 — MANIFESTING WITH THE MONTHS

19   January

21   February

25   March

29   April

31   May

35   June

39   July

43   August

47   September

51   October

55   November

59   December

SECTION 2 — MANIFESTING WITH THE COSMIC EVENTS

67   Spring Equinox

73   Fall Equinox

77   Summer Solstice

79   Winter Solstice

81   Eclipses

93   Sirius Gateway

97   Lionsgate Gateway

101   Merkaba Portal

105   Retrogrades

SECTION 3 — MANIFESTING WITH THE PLANETS

111   Connecting with Your Planet

117   Sun

121   Moon

125   Mercury

129   Venus

133   Mars

137   Jupiter

141   Saturn

145   Uranus

149   Neptune

153   Pluto

157   Chiron

SECTION 4 — MANIFESTING WITH THE ASTROLOGICAL SIGNS

165   Aries

169   Taurus

173   Gemini

177   Cancer

181   Leo

185   Virgo

189   Libra

193   Scorpio

197   Sagittarius

201   Capricorn

205   Aquarius

209   Pisces

SECTION 5 — MANIFESTING WITH THE MOON

213   The Moon

217   Working With The Cycles of the Moon

219   Enhancing Your Moon Connection

223   Harnessing the Moon Cycles for Manifesting

231   Moon Cycle Manifesting Guidesheet

249   Moon Magic and the Zodiac

255   Moon in Aries

265   Moon in Taurus

273   Moon in Gemini

279   Moon in Cancer

285   Moon in Leo

293   Moon in Virgo

299   Moon in Libra

305   Moon in Scorpio

311   Moon in Sagittarius

317   Moon in Capricorn

323   Moon in Aquarius

329   Moon in Pisces

335   *About the Author*

The Essential Manifesting Guidebook!

First things first: if you've been on the hunt for that one perfect guide to unlock the universe's secrets, take a deep breath. You've landed in just the right cosmic corner. This isn't just any book; it's your trusty companion, whispering that with a sprinkle of stardust and a dash of belief, you can achieve anything. Remember, the universe has your back, and so do I. You've got this!

With so much love and magic swirling around, it's easy to feel a little lost sometimes. But here's the good news: manifesting isn't rocket science. It's more like a dance, and the universe is eager to be your dance partner. Whether you're a seasoned cosmic explorer or just dipping your toes into the starry waters, this guidebook is your go-to map, charting out the celestial wonders.

Think of the moonlit nights our ancestors experienced, feeling the universe's heartbeat. They had their stories painted on cave canvases; we've got the power of modern wisdom combined with ancient insights. All translated into a language of love, encouragement, and empowerment, just for you.

So, here's our shimmering journey together:

1. Dream big and from the heart.

2. Use the cosmic calendar to align with the sun, the moon, and the cosmic stars.

3. Dive deep into each chapter, absorbing the energy and insights.

4. Pick your perfect cosmic vibe, knowing the universe is cheering you on.

5. Map out your manifesting steps, either with our curated worksheets or with your own special touch.

Together, we're making this journey fun, enlightening, and oh-so-magical. Because remember, you're right where you're meant to be, and with this guidebook in hand, the universe is yours to embrace. Ready to shine bright? Let's embark on this adventure, manifesting dreams one star at a time!

A Moment Before We Dance with the Stars

It's no coincidence. Whether driven by a twinkling curiosity or a heartfelt pull, you stand at the threshold of a celestial dance that promises transformation. In the pages that lie ahead, we'll waltz with the wonders of the universe, and cha-cha with our deepest desires.

But before we embark on this starlit journey, let's take a moment.

Close your eyes. Take a deep, grounding breath. Envision your dreams, feel their weight, their warmth, their wonder. Know that they're valid, they're vibrant, and most importantly, they're very much within your reach.

Together, we'll delve into the cosmic symphony of manifesting. We'll demystify the celestial, grounding it in the science of today, and the wisdom of yesteryears. With every turn of the page, imagine you're taking a step closer to your dreams, with the universe as your dance partner, guiding and supporting you with every beat.

So, slip on your dancing shoes (or comfy reading socks!), grab a cozy blanket or a cup of tea, and let's get ready to groove. The stars are aligned, the music's about to play, and this, dear reader, is your invitation to dance.

Speak to the universe with a heart full
of trust; in its cosmic dance, your
dreams are a must.

Grooving with the Universe, Backed by Cosmic Logic

As we embark on this journey of manifesting, let's understand that you're already a natural at this! Believe it or not, every thought, every feeling, and every action you've taken up till now has been a part of your manifesting journey. Sometimes we inadvertently manifest things we don't necessarily desire, simply because that's where our focus has been. So, how about we channel that energy more purposefully?

1. **The Science of Thought:** Did you know the human brain processes around 70,000 thoughts daily? Neuroscience reveals that repetitive thoughts strengthen neural pathways. Over time, what we persistently think about and believe can shape our reality. So, why not train your brain to play your favorite tune of success and joy?

2. **Vibration and Frequency:** At an atomic level, we're all vibrating energy, just like everything around us. Quantum physics supports the idea that like energies attract. Emitting positive vibes means you're more likely to attract positive outcomes. It's scientific and spiritual at the same time! Imagine syncing with the universe's playlist of endless possibilities.

3. **Intentional Action:** Dreams get their wings with action. When you align your positive thoughts and high vibes with deliberate actions, magic happens. Studies show that simply taking a step towards your goal, however small, can create a momentum that the universe loves to support.

4. **Awareness and Gratitude:** One of the foundations of cognitive science is the power of awareness and gratitude. Regularly recognizing and appreciating what you have tunes you into a frequency of abundance. This, in turn, attracts more reasons to be grateful for.

Here's the cosmic takeaway: You're already manifesting, even if subconsciously. The universe is always listening, always responding. With a blend of intention, science-backed strategies, and a sprinkle of cosmic magic, you can deliberately dance towards your dreams.

So, whether you're wishing for twinkling stars or more grounded desires, remember, with the right steps and a little starlit guidance, the universe is ready to groove with you!

How to Use this Book

Embarking on a journey of cosmic manifestation requires clarity, intention, and alignment with the universe's energies. With every page you turn in this guidebook, you immerse yourself deeper into the art of manifesting. Think of it as your manifesting compass, an indispensable tool that amplifies your manifesting abilities the more you engage with it.

1. **Clarify Your Intentions.** Before diving in, take a moment to reflect on what you genuinely wish to manifest. Whether it's an aspiration, a dream, or a tangible goal, having clarity will enhance your manifestation journey.

2. **Tune Into the Cosmos.** Being aware of current cosmic events can profoundly influence the energies you tap into. The alignment of stars, planets, and other celestial bodies holds significant power for manifestation. Stay updated on these events. You can keep track using your personal calendar or refer to the *Essential Manifesting Cosmic Calendar*. For a deeper dive into these cosmic events and their significance, visit www.shineandalignwithtrish.com.

3. **Chart Your Monthly Cosmic Energy Plan:** This plan serves as your cosmic blueprint for the month. By filling it out, you'll gain insights into:

- The upcoming cosmic events and their associated energies.

- The manifesting potential of each event.

- A range of manifesting ideas and activities tailored to each event.

4. With this knowledge in hand, you can strategically decide which manifesting techniques resonate most with you, giving you a bespoke experience tailored to your unique desires and the universe's rhythm.

5. **Manifest Anytime:** Remember, there's no strict timeline for manifestation. Anytime you feel the urge to manifest, consult this guide. Dive into its insights, read up on the current cosmic strategies, and apply them. The universe is always listening, always responsive.

6. **Stay Open and Receptive:** Manifestation is as much about sending out intentions as it is about receiving cosmic signals. Trust the process, the universe's wisdom, and most importantly, your intuition. The signs and synchronicities will guide you.

7. **Reflect and Adjust:** At each month's end, pause to reflect. Assess the energies you've harnessed, the manifestations you've experienced, and recalibrate your intentions if needed.

Remember, manifesting isn't restricted to specific times or dates. The universe is always listening, always responding. Anytime you feel called to, revisit this guide, read up on the strategies, and apply them.

There's magic in every moment, waiting to be tapped into. With this guidebook by your side, the cosmos becomes an open field of possibilities, waiting for you to sow the seeds of your dreams. Embrace this journey with an open heart and a curious mind.

Here's to a fulfilling journey of manifesting, guided by the stars and your own inner light.

For example:

It's January and you want to manifest more money.

1. Have your *Monthly Cosmic Energy Plan* handy so you can note the current energies.

2. Go to the current month on your calendar for the month's overall cosmic events. (This is the January from the *Essential Manifesting Cosmic Calendar*).

3. Note the cosmic events:

   a. *Astrological Signs:* Capricorn and Aquarius.

   b. *Moon Phases:* The month begins with Last Quarter energy, New Moon in Capricorn, First Quarter right before entering into Aquarius, and a Full Moon in Leo. (Last Quarter doesn't happen until February.)

   c. *Retrogrades:* There are 2 current retrogrades and both are going direct: Mercury (on the 1st of the month so you'll really only be working with the post shadow period) and Uranus at the end of the month.

   d. *Portals:* There are 3.

   e. *Other Cosmic Events:* None. (No eclipses, gateways, solstices)

4. Next, research each event.

   a. Flip to *Astrology Section.* Read about Capricorn and their manifesting strengths and tips. Do the same for Aquarius.

b. Next, go to the *Moon Section*. Read about each moon phase. Consider how you'd like to use them.

c. Now, look at the *Moon Magic and the Zodiac*. Read through the tips and rituals for the new and full moons. (You can also refer back to the Astrology Signs for more insight!)

5. Gather the notes you've just accumulated and decide how you want to apply them to your manifesting intention of making more money. Write this on your *Monthly Cosmic Energy Plan*. Stay open to your intuitive nudges! As you're reading, you'll intuitively sense additional ideas.

- *Capricorn is a Cardinal sign. They're great at initiating new projects. Capricorn is hard-working and a planner. This energy can help create the steps to manifest and the tenacity fortitude to manifest.*

- *Aquarius is a Fixed sign. They are the doers. Aquarius energy will provide out-of-the-box ideas. Aquarius is ruled by Uranus so there's going to be added innovative ideas for making the big bucks!*

- *The New Moon brings heightened new seeds of income. Setting the intention to bring in new prosperity!*

- *Mercury is going direct at the beginning of the month, so remembering success of the past will be easier at the beginning of the month and dwindle as the month progresses. Time for recall!*

- *Uranus goes direct at the end of the month, meanwhile, Uranus retrograde is helping recall previous times when out-of-comfort zone actions met with successful endings.*

- *On the three Angel Portal days, I'm going to set my notifications and alarms and ask angels for more guidance and help.*

MONTHLY COSMIC ENERGY PLAN

Month _____

I am Manifesting _____

Cosmic Manifesting Energies: Page #

Astrological Signs -

_____   _____

New Moon

_____   _____

Full Moon

_____   _____

Other events to note. (Retrogrades, cosmic events)

                                                                    F.I.T.

Manifesting energies I want to apply

_____
_____

My action plan -

_____
_____
_____
_____
_____
_____
_____
_____

ESSENTIAL MANIFESTING

Month ___*January*___

I am Manifesting ___*More money.*_____

_____

Cosmic Manifesting Energies: Page #

  Astrological Signs -
    ___*Capricorn & Aquarius*___   _____

  New Moon -
  ___*in Capricorn on 2nd & Aquarius on 31st*___   _____

  Full Moon -
  ___*in Capricorn on 2nd & Aquarius on 31st*___   _____

  Other events to note - (retrogrades, cosmic events)

Uranus & Venus go direct, Mercury goes Retrograde

                                    F.I.T.

Manifesting energies I want to apply -

Venus Retrograde, Uranus going direct, New Supermoon in Capricorn and

_____

I am attracting and receiving an abundance of money.

My action plan -

___*Print my calendar download included in my bonus from buying the book.*___

___*Use Venus to remember when money seemed to flow and to remind myself that I'm worthy.*___

___*Apply Uranus advice to expect the unexpected to stay manifesting money. Do a 3 moon manifesting tips.*___

_____

_____

_____

_____

_____

ESSENTIAL MANIFESTING

A full-size version of the Monthly Cosmic Energy Plan is included as your bonus for purchasing the book. To access, go to my website www.essentialmanifestingguidebook.com and put in your order number. The downloads will be sent to you right away via email.

Manifesting
WITH THE
Months

★

As the wheel of the year turns, every month showers us with its unique manifesting energy and intention. Like a cosmic timetable, this section provides you with a guide to the potent dates and phases of each month. Armed with this knowledge, you can align and amplify your manifesting endeavors, ensuring you're in rhythm with the universe's ebb and flow. Let's journey through the months, embracing their distinct vibes and making the most of each moment!

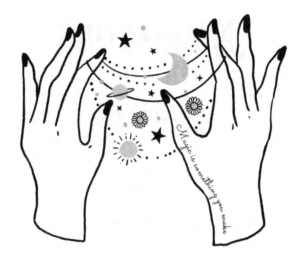

Magic is something you make

"Believe in the power within you, and
the universe will believe in your
visions too."

Months and Their Manifesting Energies

Every month arrives with its own palette of energies, rhythms, and cosmic events, painting the skies with unique patterns and offering us a chance to align our intentions in harmony. As we journey through the year, each month becomes a chapter in our manifesting story, providing distinct opportunities and challenges.

In this section, you'll be delving deep into each month's manifesting energies—those vibrant forces that set the tone for your aspirations and desires. From the passionate flames of vitality to the soft whispers of romance and the bubbling springs of joy, these energies will guide you, empowering your intentions.

But the universe doesn't stop there! You're also bestowed with special manifesting events throughout the months—cosmic waltzes that beckon you to join in. These celestial dances are pivotal moments, amplifying your connection to the vast cosmos and intensifying our manifesting powers.

Then, there are the portal days—days that are like windows to the universe, channeling intensified energies and offering us gateways to accelerated manifestation. On these days, the veil between realms thins, allowing for profound insights and spiritual connections.

And nature? It's our steadfast ally. The month's flowers for each month bloom and thrive, their petals pulsating with the manifesting energies. These floral companions, with their hues and fragrances, serve as earthly reminders of the abundant universe that surrounds us. Please incorporate them into your manifesting practice.

So, as you embark on this monthly voyage, embrace the magic, harness the energies, and dance in tune with the universe. Welcome to your monthly manifesting guide!

BE A SEEKER OF EVERYDAY *Magic*

JANUARY FLOWERS

Carnation

Love & Distinction

Snowdrop

Hope & New Beginnings

January

MANIFESTING ENERGY:

New beginnings, Working with Angels

SIGN:

Capricorn/Aquarius

MANIFESTING EVENTS

PORTAL DAYS: 1, 10, 11 bring heightened angel communication

PORTAL MANIFESTING IDEAS:

Hot Cocoa Manifestation: Enjoy a warm cup of hot cocoa while visualizing your desires as marshmallows melting into the cocoa. Sip it slowly, feeling each sip bringing your manifestations closer to reality.

Sweater Weaving Ritual: Knit or weave a cozy winter sweater or scarf. With each stitch, infuse your desires into your creation. Imagine that, like the fabric, your manifestations are being woven together.

Letter to Archangel Gabriel: Write a heartfelt letter to Archangel Gabriel, expressing your desires and goals for the new year. Ask for guidance and assistance in achieving these aspirations.

Divine Music Playlist: Create a playlist of songs that resonate with you and your manifestations. Listen to it daily and imagine your angels guiding your thoughts and communication toward your success.

FEBRUARY FLOWERS

Violet

Modesty & Spiritual Wisdom

Primrose

Youth & New Beginnings

February

MANIFESTING ENERGY:

Mystical, Loving, Partnerships

SIGN:

Aquarius/Pisces

MANIFESTING EVENTS

PORTAL DAYS: 2, 12, 20, 22 brings new partnerships with spirit guides: angels, fairies, ascended masters, goddesses, power animals, mermaids

PORTAL MANIFESTING IDEAS:

Fairy Lights Magic: Hang fairy lights in your bedroom or a cozy space. Every night, sit in the soft glow of the lights and visualize your dreams and desires as if they're sparkling around you.

Heart-Shaped Meditation: Find a heart-shaped object or picture and use it as a focal point during your daily meditation. Imagine the heart representing the love and abundance flowing into your life.

Love Letter to Yourself: Write a love letter to yourself, highlighting all your positive qualities and expressing self-love. Seal it in an envelope, place it somewhere special, and open it at the end of the month as a reminder of your self-worth.

Ocean-Infused Crystal Grid: Create a crystal grid using ocean-colored stones like aquamarine and blue calcite. Place a mermaid figurine or image in the center. Meditate by the grid and visualize the mermaids working their magic through the crystals to manifest your dreams.

Mermaid Song Affirmations: Sing or hum your favorite tunes while focusing on your desires. Imagine that your voice is a mermaid's song, enchanting the universe and calling your desires to you.

Fairy Tale Costume Ritual: Dress up in a fairy-themed costume or clothing that makes you feel magical. Spend the day in this attire and visualize yourself living your manifested desires while embracing the fairy energy within you.

Sacred Symbol Manifestation: Choose a symbol that resonates with your goals. Meditate on it and imagine it glowing with the energy of your spirit guides. Visualize this symbol helping to manifest your desires. Look for this symbol throughout your day.

*"Whisper your dreams to the fairies
at night; they'll weave them into
the morning light."*

MARCH FLOWERS

———

Daffodil
New Beginnings, Rebirth & Hope

Jonquil (type of Daffodil)
New Beginnings & Spring

March

MANIFESTING ENERGY:

Powerful & Gentle, Good Luck, Swift Shifts

SIGN:

Pisces/Aries

MANIFESTING EVENTS

EQUINOX: The Equinox occurs on the 19th. This is the Spring for the northern hemisphere and the Fall Equinox for the southern hemisphere.* (Consult the *Cosmic Events* chapter for more details)

PORTAL DAYS: 3, 13, 30 brings heightened ascended masters' energy

PORTAL MANIFESTING IDEAS:

Lucky March Charm: Create or find a lucky charm or trinket that represents your goals for the month. Carry it with you as a symbol of your manifesting intentions.

Irish Blessing Ritual: Find or create an Irish blessing that resonates with your manifesting intentions. Recite it daily as a way to invoke positive energy and good fortune.

Rainbow Visualization: Sit quietly outdoors and visualize a beautiful rainbow arching across the sky. Imagine that each color represents a different aspect of your desires coming into your life.

Ascended Master Mandalas: Create your own mandalas inspired by the colors and symbols associated with specific Ascended Masters. Coloring these mandalas can be a meditative way to connect with their energies.

Ascended Master Affirmation Cards: Make your own deck of affirmation cards, each featuring a different Ascended Master. Pull a card daily and work with the specific Master's energy to manifest your goals.

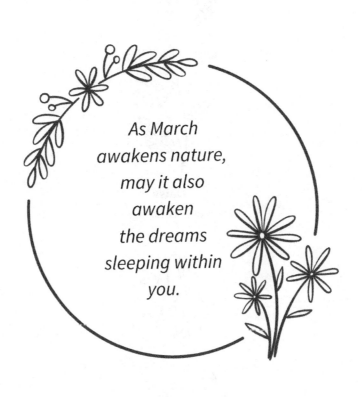

*As March
awakens nature,
may it also
awaken
the dreams
sleeping within
you.*

APRIL FLOWERS

———

Daisy
Innocence & Loyal Love

Sweet Peas
Blissful Pleasure & Gratitude

April

MANIFESTING ENERGY:
Beauty, Love, Fertility

SIGN:
Aries/Taurus

MANIFESTING EVENTS

PORTAL DAYS: 4, 14, brings heightened angel communication and connection

PORTAL MANIFESTING IDEAS:

Fruitful Abundance: Purchase or pick fresh fruits that are in season in April. Enjoy them mindfully, savoring each bite. With each taste, express gratitude for the abundance in your life and visualize your goals ripening and becoming fruitful.

Wind Chime Manifestation: Hang wind chimes outside your home or in a window. Each time the wind makes them chime, see it as a message from the universe, signaling that your manifestations are on their way.

Love Affirmations and Incense: Choose several affirmations related to love, such as *"I am deserving of love," "I attract loving relationships,"* or *"I am open to giving and receiving love."* Light a pink or green incense stick or use essential oils associated with love like rose or jasmine. Repeat your chosen affirmations while inhaling the soothing scent of the incense. Feel the presence of Archangel Chamuel supporting you as you affirm your intentions for love and harmonious relationships.

Rose Quartz Crystal Ritual: Hold a rose quartz in your hand and say, *"Archangel Chamuel, please infuse this crystal with your loving energy."* Place the crystal under your pillow or carry it with you throughout the day. As you interact with the crystal, feel the love and guidance of Archangel Chamuel filling your heart and radiating outwards.

MAY FLOWERS

Lily of the Valley
Sweetness & Luck

Hawthorn
Optimism & Joy

May

MANIFESTING ENERGY:
Fertility, Celebration, Blooming

SIGN:
Taurus/Gemini

MANIFESTING EVENTS

PORTAL DAYS: 5, 15 power days for welcoming change

PORTAL MANIFESTING IDEAS:

Dew Blessings: Dip your fingers into the morning dew from leaves first thing in the morning. Use this to anoint your forehead, visualizing the fresh, pure energy enhancing your clarity and manifesting vibrancy.

Butterfly Visualization: Butterflies are abundant in May. Watch them flutter and imagine your desires being carried on their wings, bringing change, transformation, and fruition to your intentions.

May Flower Focus: Sit comfortably in front of a Lily of the Valley or Hawthorn. Allow the flower's essence and beauty to fill your thoughts. Ask the flower to assist you in manifesting your desires, absorbing its energy and essence during your meditation. Water it as you offer it gratitude for its help.

Tree Blessing: Find a tree that speaks to you, preferably one in bloom during May. Offer it a small gift, such as a crystal, a ribbon, or some birdseed, as a token of gratitude. Sit under the tree and meditate, asking for its wisdom and guidance in manifesting your desires. Listen for any intuitive insights that may come to you.

Butterfly Transformation: Research which butterflies are common in your region during May and identify one with symbolic meaning related to transformation. Create a small butterfly-friendly garden in your yard or a pot on your balcony with flowers that attract these butterflies. As you care for the garden, visualize your own transformation and growth in alignment with the butterfly's symbolism.

YOU ARE MADE OF STARDUST AND WISHES AND MAGICAL THINGS

JUNE FLOWERS

———

Rose

Love, Passion, & Beauty

Honeysuckle

Love & Connection

June

MANIFESTING ENERGY:
Vitality, Romance, Joy

SIGN:
Gemini/Cancer

MANIFESTING EVENTS

SOLSTICE: This month celebrates a solstice! This is the Summer Solstice for the northern hemisphere and the Winter Solstice for the southern hemisphere. (For more details, consult the *Cosmic Events* chapter.)

PORTAL DAYS: 6, 16 brings an energy of harmony and balance

PORTAL MANIFESTING IDEAS:

Mirror Affirmations: Look into a mirror and speak affirmations of love and joy to yourself. "I am vibrant. I am loved. I am joyful."

Berry Blessings: June is a month of berry harvests. Create a fruit salad using different berries, each representing a different desire. As you eat, visualize each berry infusing you with the power to manifest.

Harmonic Sound Bath: Organize a personal sound bath using singing bowls, chimes, or tuning forks. As the harmonious waves wash over you, visualize your desires in perfect balance, each resonating at its unique frequency in harmony with the universe.

Balance Stone Ritual: Collect an odd number of stones from a nearby natural source. Stack them carefully, finding the perfect balance. As you do so, imagine you're aligning your intentions, one atop the other, in perfect harmony with your goals.

Twin Flame Candle Dance: Light two candles side by side, representing the duality of your intentions. Watch as the flames dance in harmony. Take a moment to write down two corresponding desires (e.g., professional success and personal relaxation). As the wax melts, visualize these desires coming into alignment, supporting and enhancing one another.

With the solstice's golden hue, may every dream and intention you've sown come true.

JULY FLOWERS

———

Larkspur
Carefree & Loving

Waterlily
Rebirth, Purity, & Enlightenment

July

MANIFESTING ENERGY:
Independence, Spiritual, Personal Power

SIGN:
Cancer/Leo

MANIFESTING EVENTS

GATEWAYS: Sirius Gateway 3 July – 7 July and Lionsgate Gateway begins 28 July. (For more details, consult the *Cosmic Events* chapter.)

PORTAL DAYS: 7, 17 brings attainment

PORTAL MANIFESTING IDEAS:

Sundress/Sunhat Dance: Don a summery outfit and dance under the sun, letting its warmth and light fill you with energy and positivity, radiating your intentions out into the world.

Gateway Journaling: Write your manifestations on paper infused with blue ink. Imagine each word being encoded with the potent energy of the Sirius Gateway.

Sacred Geometry Sigils: Draw or trace the Flower of Life or other sacred geometries. Infuse your intention into the pattern, knowing that these shapes hold the codes of creation, amplified by Sirius energy.

Crystal Constellation Grid: Create a crystal grid using stones associated with star energy, like selenite or lapis lazuli. Place them in a pattern representing the constellation of Canis Major, where Sirius is located.

Ancient Egyptian Ritual: Given the significance of Sirius in ancient Egyptian culture, honor their practices by creating a small altar with symbols like the Ankh or Eye of Horus. Light a blue candle and meditate on its flame, asking for guidance and clarity in your manifestations.

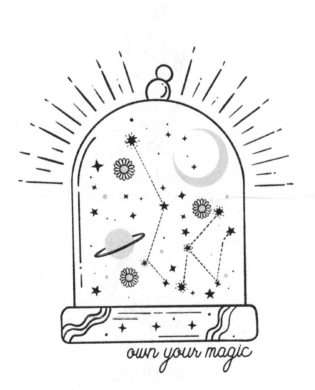

own your magic

AUGUST FLOWERS

Gladiolus

Strength & Resilience

Poppy

Imagination & Dreams

August

MANIFESTING ENERGY:
Manifesting, Harvest, Gratitude

SIGN:
Leo/Virgo

MANIFESTING EVENTS

This is a month full of manifesting. The vibration of the month is an 8!

GATEWAY: We enter this manifesting month in the flow of Lionsgate Gateway (which began on 28th July and goes through the 12th) and the Lionsgate Portal occurring on the 8th. (For more details, consult the *Cosmic Events* chapter.)

PORTAL DAYS: 8th Mega manifesting on Lionsgate Portal, 18

PORTAL MANIFESTING IDEAS:

Lion's Roar Release: Head outside and let out a cathartic roar! Feel the energy of the lion flow through you, releasing any inhibitions and making space for your intentions.

Star Sirius Visualization: Dedicate time to meditate, connecting with the star Sirius, the shining beacon during Lionsgate. Imagine its bright, blue-white light illuminating your desires, making them more vibrant and attainable.

Fiery Mane Dance: Play some tribal or high-energy music and dance like no one's watching. Imagine you have a lion's mane, flowing and radiant, symbolizing your own power and strength.

Golden Gateway Craft: Using golden paper or cardboard, craft a mini 'gateway'. Write down your desires and pass them through your gateway, symbolizing their journey from intention to reality.

Jungle Drumming: Use a drum or a simple hand tapping rhythm to sync with the heartbeats of lions. Feel the resonance with the majestic energies, charging your manifestations.

Lion's Mane Flower Crown: Craft a floral crown, symbolizing the majestic mane of a lion. As you wear it, feel the royalty and prowess of the lion, boosting your confidence in your manifesting journey.

Feline Friendship: Spend a day with cats or feline creatures. Observe their regality and confidence. Let it inspire you to adopt similar energies in your manifesting process.

Golden Crystal Meditation: Use golden or sun-colored crystals like citrine or sunstone. Meditate with them during the August Portals, and Lionsgate peak, imagining a golden light amplifying your desires.

With the Lionsgate as your guiding light, move forward with courage, passion, and might.

SEPTEMBER FLOWERS

Aster

Love, Wisdom, & Faith

Morning Glory

Love & Affection

September

MANIFESTING ENERGY:

Goddess Energy, Transformation, Growth

SIGN:

Virgo/Libra

MANIFESTING EVENTS

EQUINOX: The Equinox occurs on the 23rd. This is the Fall for the northern hemisphere and Spring Equinox for the southern hemisphere. (For more details, consult the *Cosmic Events* chapter.)

PORTAL DAYS: 9, 19 brings heightened goddess energy

PORTAL MANIFESTING IDEAS:

Here are creative ways to harness these energies:

Goddess Garments: Dress up in clothes or jewelry that makes you feel divine, powerful, and goddess-like. Embrace that energy throughout your day. With every step you take radiate confidence, knowing you are gorgeous, brilliant, and sassilicious. Allow this energy to enhance your intentions and manifesting energies.

Goddess Vision Board: Craft a vision board focused solely on goddess energy. Use images, symbols, and affirmations that resonate with the divine feminine and inspire you.

Moonstone Magic: Moonstone channels goddess energy. Hold one and meditate on your desires, imagining the goddess energy within amplifying your intentions.

Goddess Bath: Create a luxurious bath with rose petals, honey, and milk. As you soak, envision the nurturing goddess energy cleansing and empowering your manifestations.

Goddess Affirmations: Write affirmations that align with your goddess energy, such as *"I am powerful and divine, channeling the goddess from within."*

Goddess Candle Magic: Carve symbols or words representing your desires into a candle. As you light it, imagine the flame as the goddess's spirit, helping to manifest and illuminate your path forward.

Earthly Perfume Potion: Virgo is an earth sign, and who better to channel than the goddess herself? Forage or select herbs like lavender or rosemary. Mix them with earthy essential oils like patchouli or cedarwood in a small vial. Whenever you need a boost, dab a little on your wrists, and let the Virgo goddess energy envelop you.

Craft a Goddess Amulet: Create or buy a pendant that represents the goddess. Wear it close to your heart, using it as a touchstone for your intentions.

OCTOBER FLOWERS

—

Marigold
Warmth & Creativity

Cosmos
Balance, Tranquility, & Harmony

October

MANIFESTING ENERGY:

Magical, New Beginnings & Endings, Manifesting

SIGN:

Libra/Scorpio

MANIFESTING EVENTS

This month is also a powerful manifesting energy. Octo is derived from the Latin word for 8. The 10 brings endings and new beginnings.

The veil continues to thin this month until fully exposed on the 31st. This is a time for celebrating our ancestors, communicating with spirit guides such as angels, fairies, and ascended masters.

PORTAL DAYS: 8, 10, 18 for manifesting new

PORTAL MANIFESTING IDEAS:

Pumpkin Seed Wishes: Carve out a pumpkin and as you remove the seeds, whisper a wish into each one. Plant them in your garden or a pot, envisioning your desires growing with them.

Witchy Wind Chimes: Create wind chimes using objects that resonate and represent your desires. Hang them by your window and every time they chime, imagine your intentions resonating throughout the universe.

Broomstick Clearing: Take a broomstick (or a regular broom) and sweep around your house, especially the entrance. As you do, chant an affirmation about clearing old energy and making way for new manifestations.

Cauldron Manifestation: Use a pot or bowl as your 'cauldron'. Fill it with water and drop shiny coins into it while saying your intentions. Stir it in a clockwise motion to amplify its energy.

Oracle Intention Setting: Pull an Oracle card each morning. Let it guide your focus and intention for the day, drawing you closer to your desires. (If using my Essential Manifesting Oracle Deck then make the most of the accompanying guidebook for more manifesting magic!)

Potion Brewing: Make a special tea blend representing your desires. As you sip, visualize the warm drink energizing your intentions from within.

October Leaf Notes: Write your desires on fallen autumn leaves with a gold pen. Release them in a flowing stream or river, visualizing them carrying your intentions into the universe.

Enchanted Mirror Talk: Talk to your reflection in a mirror by candlelight. Speak about your future as if it's already happening. The mirror amplifies and reflects your intentions back to you.

ALWAYS BELIEVE IN *Magic*

NOVEMBER FLOWERS

———

Chrysanthemum
Friendship & Joy

Peony
Prosperity & Passion

November

MANIFESTING ENERGY:
Gratitude, Angels, Abundance

SIGN:
Scorpio/Sagittarius

MANIFESTING EVENTS

PORTAL DAYS: 1,10, 11 for manifesting with angels and clear angel communication

PORTAL MANIFESTING IDEAS:

Angels will always help you with your manifesting, so deepening your relationship with angels on Portal Days makes angel communication even easier. Here are a couple ideas:

Angel Doodles: Whenever you have a free moment, doodle angel wings, halos, or any other symbols related to angels. Keep a dedicated 'Angel Journal' for these sketches.

Feather Hunt: Head out for a walk and look for feathers. Every feather you find could be a sign or message from your angels. Turn it into a game, asking angels for hints and trying to find them!

Angel Jewelry: Wearing angel-themed jewelry, like angel wing necklaces or guardian angel pendants, can serve as a physical reminder of their presence.

Affirmations: Create a set of angelic affirmations and recite them throughout the day. For example: *"I am always surrounded by angelic love and protection."*

Winged Crafts: Spend an afternoon creating crafts with an angel theme, such as angelic bookmarks, winged jewelry, or heavenly wall art. As you craft, open yourself up to hearing your guardian angel's messages and inspiration.

Angelic Dreamcatcher: Craft a dreamcatcher, but with an angelic twist. Decorate it with white feathers, star-shaped beads, and shimmering threads. Hang it near your bed to invite angelic dreams and guidance at night.

Scented Connection: Use essential oils like frankincense, myrrh, or rose to create an angelic atmosphere. Diffuse them in your living space and set the intention to heighten your angelic connection whenever you smell them.

Angel Playlist: Create a music playlist filled with songs that remind you of angels or make you feel closer to the divine. Play it during moments of reflection or when you just want to feel their presence.

*Angels wrap your dreams in divine
light, ensuring they manifest
beautifully and right.*

DECEMBER FLOWERS

Narcissus

Rebirth, Hope, & Fresh Starts

Holly

Protection & Happiness

December

MANIFESTING ENERGY:

Divine Guidance, Vibrational Increase, Transformation

SIGN:

Sagittarius/Capricorn

MANIFESTING EVENTS

PORTALS: 12 December through 21 is the Merkaba Gateway, 12 December is the Merkaba Portal (For more details, consult the *Cosmic Events* chapter.)

SOLSTICES: This month celebrates a solstice on the 21st! This is the Winter Solstice for the northern hemisphere and the Summer Solstice for the southern hemisphere. (For more details, consult the *Cosmic Events* chapter.)

PORTAL DAYS: 12 for manifesting, spiritual upgrade, healing and working with Archangel Metatron

PORTAL MANIFESTING IDEAS:

Get twelve small white candles, a piece of paper, a gold pen, and a clear quartz crystal.

Begin by drawing a large star on the paper with your gold pen. This star represents Archangel Metatron's energy and the portal.

Write down a manifesting intention or wish inside each point of the star. These represent the 12 magic moments of the portal day.

Place the clear quartz crystal in the center of the star. This acts as a beacon to amplify your intentions with Archangel Metatron's guidance.

Arrange the twelve white candles around the paper, forming a circle.

Light each candle, starting from the topmost point of the star and moving clockwise. As you light them, recite: *"With Metatron's light, my wishes take flight. Through this portal, my intentions ignite."*

Spend a few moments in quiet reflection. Envision your wishes coming true and feel the energy of the December 12 portal enveloping you.

Once done, safely extinguish the candles. Keep the star paper and crystal in a special place for the rest of the month.

Add the flowers of the month for its energetic boost.

Remember, December's Portal Day is a potent time for spiritual growth, healing, and manifesting your desires. Harness this energy, and let Archangel Metatron guide you through this magical journey!

Manifesting
WITH THE
Cosmic Events

Throughout the year, the cosmos treats us to special events, each pulsing with unique energy and offering manifesting shortcuts. Think of these events as your cosmic upgrades. When you intentionally tap into these celestial happenings, you're supercharging your manifesting journey. Here you'll learn to sync with the celestial rhythms and harness these cosmic currents for manifesting magic!

*When you align your inner energies
with your goals, the universe
conspires in your favor.*

Meanings & Manifesting

Cosmic events are like the universe's own fireworks show—bursting with vibrant, escalated surges of energy. Think of them as the universe's way of giving you a spiritual high-five. The best part? You don't even have to lift a finger to receive this astral upgrade. Just by being, you're getting a dash of positive cosmic glitter.

But ah, knowledge is power! By tuning into these celestial shindigs and understanding their rhythm, you can ride the cosmic waves like a pro surfer. Let's break it down:

Cosmic events covered in this section:

- **Equinox:** The universe's great balancers! Picture the sun doing a tightrope walk right over the equator, giving both hemispheres a wink with equal day and night. Spring equinox is Mother Nature's gentle nudge saying, "Wakey-wakey!", while Fall equinox is her soothing lullaby, prepping us for the cozy times ahead. Truly, nature's equilibrium extravaganza!

- **Solstice:** The universe's biannual stretch! Imagine the sun pulling a yoga pose, leaning as far away from the equator as it can get, giving us the longest and shortest days of the year. Summer solstice is the sun's show-off day, while winter solstice is its cozy blanket moment.

- **Eclipses:** The universe's wildcards! Just when you thought you had it all figured out, along comes an eclipse with a surprise twist, opening doors to unforeseen opportunities.

  > *Solar Eclipse* is when Earth slips into the moon's shadow. In manifesting, Solar Eclipse impacts physical and external manifesting.

  > *Lunar Eclipse* is when the moon slips into the Earth's shadow. In manifesting, Lunar Eclipse impacts emotional and spiritual manifesting.

- **Gateway/Portals:** Think of these as the universe's secret passages, each one holding a different key that unlocks incredible manifesting mojo.

  > *Sirius Gateway* is an annual event when our sun's older, big brother, Sirius is closest to Earth. Sirius is known as our spiritual sun.

  > *Lionsgate Gateway/Portal* is an annual event when manifesting is markedly escalated.

  > *Merkaba Portal* is a time for upgrading your vibration with the Divine Light. This portal opens on the 12th of December and completes its upgrade on the Winter Solstice.

- **Retrogrades:** Often given the side-eye, these phases are actually your spiritual pit stops. A time to reflect, reassess, and refine your dreams and desires. Retrograde dates are included in this chapter, while manifesting with each planet's retrograde is included in the *Planet* chapter.

Using these cosmic events

Cosmic events bring an escalated and powerful surge of energy. Actually, you don't even have to do anything to receive the spiritual upgrade. You will receive a positive vibrational boost just from the event. However, you will benefit exponentially by knowing about the event and determining how you want to apply its energies.

For manifesting, review the purpose of each and how to incorporate into the outcome you want.

1. Identify how you wish to use the event.

2. Work through the provided steps or create your own manifesting routine.

3. Mark your calendar. Set your alarm. Schedule and create a plan how you want to use each cosmic event.

*With love as your guide and faith
as your compass, may everything
you manifest be precious and
wondrous.*

Spring Equinox

Northern Hemisphere occurs anywhere from 19 - 21 March
Southern Hemisphere occurs anywhere from 21 - 24 September

$\mathcal{S}$ pring Equinox is the time of year when the day is the same length as the night. Talk about balance!

The energy of new growth, rebirth and awakening is happening in nature and within our homes.

What would you like to welcome in and manifest into your life during this season of hope, fertility and growth?

You can plant seeds, walk in nature, and do stretches, or yoga.

This is also a natural time for spring cleaning and preparing your home for welcoming new manifesting energies.

How to Use the Spring Equinox

1. Clean a Room

*This can be your most used room, office, or sacred space.**

1) Set your intention for this space to be completely cleared of the old, lingering, stagnant energies and revitalized with the new, vibrant spring energies. By cleaning your area your actions are removing

any blocking or limiting manifesting energies and creating space for to welcome in the new!

2) Tidy the area. Give away or toss items that you intuitively sense need to be removed or donated.

3) Clean the space. Dust, vacuum, and wash any mirrors or surfaces. While doing this visualize sunbeams of energy, joy, and love filling the space.

Create your own cleanser by adding two drops of your favorite essential oil* to your one cup vinegar, one cup water solution for added benefits. Pet friendly and good for cleaning essential oils are frankincense, lemongrass, and arborvitae. *Always research essential oils to ensure their safety.*

4) Bless your space. You can say your own or use this one.

Springtime Space-Cleansing & Manifestation Blessing

"Freshly swept, clutter cleared, space divine,
With this spring cleaning, let my sanctuary shine.
Gone is the old, making way for the new,
As spring's manifesting energies flow and ensue.

Sunlight beams, gentle breezes blow,
In this refreshed space, may positivity grow.
With every nook cleansed and every corner free,
I call upon the universe, aligning my desires with thee.

Spring's renewing spirit, both near and afar,
Guide my intentions, let them shine like a star.
As flowers bloom and birds begin to sing,
May this space reflect the magic and abundance spring brings!"

What's A Sacred Space?

It's a place of tranquility and purpose: it could be a dedicated room, a serene corner, or even a thoughtful windowsill arrangement. This space is adorned with meaningful trinkets, crystals, and cherished photos. You might also find essential oils that you want to add to provide a sense of peace, or select objects that resonate with personal significance, or candles that lend their energies.

More than just a physical spot, it's a dedicated area for reflection and connection. Within its boundaries, distractions fade, allowing for a deep, spiritual communion. This is your personal haven, where introspection is embraced, and the daily hustle is momentarily set aside.

2. *Make a Springtime Wreath.*

MATERIALS:

- Grapevine or wreath frame (available at craft stores or if you're handy you can create)
- Spring colored ribbons
- Fresh or faux spring flowers (daffodils, tulips, lily of the valley, primroses)
- Fresh or faux greenery (eucalyptus, grasses)
- Hot glue gun (optional)
- Floral wire (optional)
- Scissors (optional)
- Decorative elements (birds, eggs, fairies, lamb, and anything you connect with spring time)
- Spring colored ribbons

  Pink – optimism and love
  Green - hope, new life

Yellow – creativity and joy
Purple – mystery and wisdom
White – new beginnings and innocence

DIRECTIONS:

1) Prepare your items that you want to use. For example, make sure no bugs or any unwanted things are on the fresh flowers.

2) Attach the greenery and flowers to your wreath. Glue or use floral wire if needed.

3) Add your decorative elements. Glue or use floral wire to attach firmly if needed.

4) Attach or wrap your desired ribbons around your wreath.

5) Bless your wreath when done and hang on your front door to welcome in the new, positive energies.

You can say your own blessing or use this one.

Springtime Wreath Blessing

Whimsical flowers, colors so bright,
Bless this wreath with pure delight.
As springtime energies dance in the breeze,
May we harness their power with grace and ease.
With each bloom and twist of vine,
May manifesting blessings forever intertwine.
Welcoming abundance, joy, and all things divine,
With this wreath, let our intentions align.
Through laughter, hope, and the sun's warm caress,
May our spring be filled with love and success!

3. Draw an Egg Mandala

MATERIALS:

- Paper
- Pencil
- Colored pencils
- Red candle
- Matches

1) Draw a large egg on your paper. Egg is the symbol for life. This represents the dream you're ready to manifest.

2) Within the egg, draw the outcome you desire* as if it's already attained. This is a focused space for your manifestation to Spring forth.

   Manifesting Tip: Hand draw this image. Do not print out an image. This is to come from you as part of YOUR creation. You do not need to be an artist. You just need to set the intention for what you draw to come true.

3) Add colors to empower your egg. Just like color therapy is used today, ancients knew the energy of color, which is why many people color eggs during Easter.

4) Once you feel your egg is complete, place your drawing in your sacred space.

5) Light a red candle.

6) Looking at your egg mandala, state your intention....

   "Today I celebrate the energy of a new cycle in the world and within me. I welcome the sun and fulfillment of the desires placed in my egg. I choose to and will take action to manifest this treasure that is aligned with my soul's path. It is with my sincerest gratitude that I welcome and honor this cycle of growth."

7) Extinguish your candle and place it by your paper. Know this red candle is like a magnet calling out to the universe and all the spiritual assistance. It says "notice me!"

8) Take a moment visualizing this image as it has manifested! Really lean into the emotions of joy, success and gratitude.

9) When you feel ready, thank your angels for providing encouragement and guidance for this manifestation.

"I am fresh like spring attracting fresh new blessings."

Fall Equinox

Northern Hemisphere occurs anywhere from 21 - 24 September

Southern Hemisphere occurs anywhere from 19 - 21 March

Fall Equinox is the other time of year when the day is the same length as the night. Another powerful time for balance!

The energy is of celebrating your harvest, gratitude, abundance, balance, and new seeds.

Just like the acorns that are snuggling into the ground, ready to grow into a humongous oak tree, this is a mighty manifesting time for your dreams ready to become reality.

How to Use the Fall Equinox

1. **Celebrate your Harvest.**

   Write down all of your successes for this year. Use front and back. This is a time of celebrating the cornucopia of overflowing blessings. Include your accomplishments. Any progress or growth is important. Remember that little acorn. It seems tiny, but that little nut on the ground is the beginning. Boast about your every accomplishment! This can be something as simple as saying a daily affirmation!

2. **Re-establish Balance.**

Draw a circle representing your favorite pie. Divide the pie into slices representing how much time, including thoughts, energy and action, is dedicated to each of the following: home, family, friends, self, work, and dreams.

Are there areas out of balance that may need tweaking prior to planting the new manifesting seeds?

3. **Plant New Seeds.**

Identify what new "seeds" to plant. What new desires or habits would you like? What do you want to plant within your soul so you will reap a healthy harvest in the Spring? Plant spring bulbs to represent these habits and desires.

4. **Express Gratitude.**

Gratitude sets the tone and vibration to receive more to be grateful for, plus studies have shared multiple health benefits! Write a letter of gratitude for your experiences over the past six months. Include successes, gifts, and anything you intuitively feel should be added. Even if it's overcoming a negative encounter or finally releasing that challenge or bad habit, share in your letter. Place somewhere safe and revisit at the Spring Equinox.

5. **Release and Let Go**

With the good, sometimes the bad has infiltrated. This can be negative thinking, feeling disheartened or just an "out with the old, in with the new" desire.

1) Title your paper with "List 1" and write a list of what needs to be released.

For example: painful memories, hurts, insecurities, doubt, misunderstanding, regrets, that thing that happened seven years ago.

2) On a fresh page, title it "List 2" and write what you desire.

   For example: dreams, goals, creating new memories, financial security, peace of mind.

3) Find a safe place to burn your lists. (I have an iron pot with a lid for indoor burning and a specific firepit for outdoors exclusively used for these types of things.)

4) Burn "List 1" saying, *"Thank you for the experience & knowledge gained. I no longer need nor benefit from holding onto these lessons. If there is still more to be understood for my soul, I will attract it in a kinder, loving way. I bless and release all attachments, identities and limitations. Thank you!"*

5) Allow burning of the list to complete before the next step.

6) Burn List 2 saying, *"Thank you for igniting these dreams & desires. I am open to receiving blessings & love for my highest good. I allow the energy of love and success to radiate from my soul. With harm to none. Thank you!"*

7) Safely ensure the fire is extinguished. Do not roast marshmallows over these ashes. Once these ashes are cooled, scatter them at the edge of your property. Wash your hands as a signal to the Universe that you know it's acting on these desires.

"I am blessed every day, in every way."

*With blessings as numerous as
solstice rays, may your
manifestations find countless ways.*

Summer Solstice

Northern Hemisphere occurs anywhere from 20 - 22 June
Southern Hemisphere occurs anywhere from 20 - 23 December

ummer Solstice shines as the day with the most sunlight. From ancient civilizations to our modern times, this luminous occasion has been celebrated with zest and zeal. Festivals and activities burst forth, echoing the jubilation of this radiant day. Think of it as nature's amplifier, taking the manifesting vibes and supercharging them. It's the universe's way of adding extra logs to your manifesting bonfire.

Use this time to activate your intentions, soak in the healing power of the sun and the positive manifesting energies and ask yourself, "What do I truly want to manifest?"

A Summer Solstice Manifesting Ritual

1. Set your alarm to wake prior to sunrise.

2. Grab paper, pencil, colored pencils, and your favorite morning beverage. *I intentionally bring my sun tea for this special morning.*

3. Snuggle into a cozy place where you'll be able to see the rising sun.

4. As the sun rises, begin creating your manifesting vision sheet.

Draw images of what you want to manifest. Use symbols or sketch images to the best of your abilities. For example, draw a heart to represent love or a treasure chest full of coins and jewels for prosperity and abundance or a smiley face representing joy for successfully manifesting all that you desire.

Write on your page, *"Thank you for this or something better."*

5. Once the sun is fully shining, hold your sheet and stand. Still holding your sheet in your left hand, raise your arms as if soaking up the morning rays and pulling in her energy.

6. Thank God and the angels for the sunshine, creating a clear path and for overseeing your dreams come true.

   You can say something like, *"Thank you for blessing my dreams. I honor and appreciate the brilliant light and heightened energy flowing to my desires during this powerful time. Thank you, God, and angels for accelerating the manifestation of these dreams fulfilled. As always, my sincere desire is for harm to none and blessings for all. Amen."*

7. Leave your paper where it will energize in the sun all day.

8. Once sun has set place your paper in your sacred space to review at Winter Solstice.

"I am radiant and beaming with manifesting energy."

Winter Solstice

Northern Hemisphere occurs anywhere from 20 - 23 December

Southern Hemisphere occurs anywhere from 20 - 22 June

The Winter Solstice, with its shortest span of daylight, serves as a powerful moment in your manifesting journey. Though the days will slowly grow longer after this point, the Winter Solstice is an invitation to journey inward. Use this as a time of introspection and deep reflection, allowing you to clarify your desires and intentions.

This gentle time is also an invitation to embrace the spirit of the solstice by acknowledging and expressing gratitude for the past year's lessons, blessings, and growth. This positive energy will propel your intentions and manifestations into the universe with greater force. You can journal to track your blessings and celebrate the solstice in any way that speaks to your soul. Here is a simple ritual that will help you shine brighter into the following year!

A Winter Solstice Manifesting Ritual

(To empower this ritual, listen to my Winter Solstice Guided Meditation on my YouTube channel or website: www.shineandalignwithtrish.com.)

MATERIALS:

- Yellow or gold candle
- Paper, pencil, and colored pencils

DIRECTIONS:

1. Light your candle.

2. Draw a large rectangle on your page.

3. Within the rectangle, create a table with 9 squares by drawing 2 horizontal and 2 vertical lines within. Just like a tic tac toe within the rectangle.

4. In the boxes draw the following symbols: evergreen tree, mistletoe & holly, star, sun, candle, snowflake, and draw a present with a bow in each of the 3 remaining squares.

5. Add color in your symbols.

   Red for strength, protection and good luck

   Green for protection prosperity and mental rejuvenations

   White for this new magical, manifesting phase, new goals and new sense of peace and bliss

   Silver for increased healing, increased clarity and heightened intuition

   Gold for accelerated success, increased abundance and happiness

6. Thank God and the angels for the warmth and every glowing flame. You can say something like, *"Thank you for wrapping my dreams and desires in the warm, loving protection. I am filled with peace and gratitude knowing these dreams have already come true and are just waiting to come to light. I honor and appreciate the manifesting energy flowing to my desires during this powerful time. Thank you, God, and angels for accelerating the manifestation of something better or these dreams fulfilled. As always, my sincere desire is for harm to none and blessings for all. Amen."*

7. Using your candle to light the way, place this in your sacred space. Extinguish your candle and place the candle on or by your sheet.

"I am a beautiful and powerful light"

Eclipses

LUNAR & SOLAR

E clipses deliver powerful and accelerated change. They pinpoint what's blocking your success in manifesting. They aren't stingy with the information either. If you ask, they will tell you. They will also provide swift, positive, manifesting change.

Working with eclipses with intention will amplify your efforts, guiding you to clear away the shadows that hold you back. Think of them as trusted mentors, always pushing you towards your highest potential. They believe in the boundless magic within you, even when you may doubt. So, embrace the transformative power of these cosmic events, lean into their wisdom, and watch as they light up the path to your dreams. With the universe by your side, you are unstoppable!

Did you know eclipses used to cause panic and fear in people as the moon or sun disappeared? The light provided by the heavenly bodies gets blocked and the sky gets dark. They thought the world was coming to an end. To this day, animals still get disoriented. They will actually do their nighttime routine during a total solar eclipse!

Likewise, you can intuitively sense the upcoming event. You can do nothing and simply allow the adjustments to play out in your life. You can, also, choose to plan around the event and make the most of this rapid impact. Changes often appear within the period of the current eclipse pair or will complete through the eclipse season.

Some things to note:

- Eclipses come in pairs.
- Eclipses provide laser focus.
- A solar eclipse always occurs with a new moon, so it will always offer impactful new beginnings.
- A lunar eclipse always occurs with a full moon, so it will always offer impactful revelations.
- Eclipses occur two to three times a year.

A *Solar Eclipse* is when Earth slips into the moon's shadow. The line-up is earth, moon, sun.

A *Lunar Eclipse* is when the moon slips into Earth's shadow. The line-up is moon, earth, sun.

An *"Almost" Eclipse* is when the Earth, Sun, and Moon are close for the alignment, but not close enough.

How does this boost your manifesting?

Solar Eclipse Energy for Manifesting

This is the time for outward changes baby! You know those action steps you've been delaying or worried about doing? This is the time to embrace the solar eclipse's energy to inspire physical transformations, external changes and initiating action steps toward manifesting your dreams.

When tuning into this solar power, think of the sun's qualities: determination, assertiveness, responsiveness, and expressiveness, all harmonizing with the yang energy of action and outward momentum.

Let the sun's radiant yang energy amplify your manifesting intentions and actions. You'll know the bold, action steps to take!

Lunar Eclipse Energy for Manifesting

Inward changes, here you come! You know those little thoughts, fears, and beliefs that might be sneaking around, trying to slow down your manifesting groove? Well, Lunar Eclipse to the rescue! This is the time to embrace the lunar eclipse's energy to inspire internal transformations and positive, mindset changes. The spiritual aspect of the moon will help you remember your divine connection. This supercharges alignment with your divine self so that you confidently know that you are deserving of manifesting your dreams.

When tuning into this lunar power, think of the moon's essence: intuition, introspection, and nurturing. Its nurturing feminine energy is all about taking a step back, understanding deeply, and getting cozy with your inner self. Time for some lunar love and self-discovery!

"Almost" Lunar Eclipse Energy for Manifesting

We can all relate to those "almost" moments. Even the Moon! It takes alignment for any eclipse to occur. The lunar eclipse happens because Earth slips right in between the sun and moon and blocks the sunlight. So an "almost" is the cosmic dance line was gathered and one was running a bit late. The eclipse doesn't happen, not even to qualify for the partial. That's okay though! The manifesting opportunities are still present.

To make the most of this time contemplate your "almost" snippets of success or areas where you're feeling "off."

Where have things not line up for you? Are you feeling like your dreams are falling behind? Are you feeling like your manifesting is close but not there?

A lunar eclipse, which can only occur during a full moon, acts as a cosmic accelerator, supercharging the energies at play and prompting profound transformations. This is a great time to ask for clarity as to why your manifesting is falling short. Ask questions like, "why am I being held back," or "what can I do to align myself with success?"

The full moon brings the light to your questions. Shadows are revealed. Your intuition is heightened so you will have the answers!

For extra manifesting ingredients, look at which Astrological sign the moon is in and blend in their strengths! This year's "almost eclipse" is in the Full Moon of Aries.

Manifesting Tip

Each eclipse occurs within an astrological sign, bringing with it a unique energy and essence. Consult the *Astrological Signs* chapter for more understanding of the underlying patterns and energies at play. Use this when creating your manifesting plan so you benefit from all eclipse energy. Your *Monthly Cosmic Energy Plan* is included in the Resource section of the book. A printable version is included as your bonus for purchasing the book. To access, go to www.essentialmanifestingguidebook.com and put in your order number. Your downloads will be sent to you right away via your email inbox.

Navigating Eclipses

Prior to the eclipse:

1. Note the current time for your location. I like the website www.timeanddate.com

2. Note the astrological sign for the eclipse and characteristics. How can you incorporate and leverage this sign's energy and strengths?

3. Identify where you'd like clarification. You'll know this area because you're already experiencing frustration around this.

4. Set your intention to receive the guidance for the transformation you desire.

5. Write your list and set it aside. For example, *"What's blocking me from financial abundance? What's blocking the love of my life? What's with this extra weight?"*

6. Throughout the day look for the revelations. You may suddenly notice signs and symbols appearing. Pay attention to this guidance. Your intuition will help identify, acknowledge and interpret the messages you receive.

7. Next, you get to decide how you want to proceed. Do you acknowledge but choose to ignore or do you commit to taking action and welcoming in the transformations? Whatever you decide is the right decision. If you want to move forward, then commit to three ways you will implement the epiphanies the eclipses provided.

8. Offer words of gratitude for the clarity. Take a cleansing breath.

Shifts will continue after the eclipse, so keep noticing the divine guidance of signs, symbols, and messages.

Lunar Eclipse Ritual

Lunar Eclipse Drawing:

The act of drawing under the gentle light of a lunar eclipse is not just an artistic endeavor, but a mystical journey. It's about capturing a fleeting celestial moment, feeling the pulse of the universe, and translating that energy onto paper.

MATERIALS:

- A sketchbook or quality drawing paper
- Pencils of varying colors
- A good eraser
- A soft pastel or watercolor set (optional, for adding touches of color)
- A cozy blanket or cushion to sit on
- A small light or candle for soft illumination (ensure it doesn't interfere with your view of the moon) I use a book light.
- If you can't get outside, find a comfy indoor spot where the moon can still be seen.
- Your favorite cup of tea or water

DIRECTIONS:

1. **Prepare Your Sacred Space:** Choose a comfortable spot with an unobstructed view of the moon. Spread your blanket or cushion, and set your materials around you. Turn on your light or light your or candle, letting its gentle glow illuminate your paper.

2. **Connect with your Canvas:** Before you start drawing, hold your sketchbook or your hands. Feel its weight, texture, and potential. This blank space is about to be imbued with both celestial and personal energies.

3. **Get Grounded:** Sit comfortably, close your eyes, and take three deep, cleansing breaths. Visualize golden roots spiraling downward from your root chakra into the earth below. Take a cleansing breath allowing yourself to feel anchored and secure. Next, visualize a silver thread from your root chakra spiraling upward connecting you to the moon above.

4. **Call In the Lunar Energy:** Open your heart to the moon by visualizing its phases, cycles, and the transformative energy of the eclipse. Whisper or think: "Moon of transformation, guide my hand and my heart in this creation."

5. **Craft Your Intention:** Reflect on what you hope to achieve with your drawing. Do you want it to be a representation of personal growth, a release of past energies, or perhaps a manifestation of future aspirations? Frame a clear and concise statement. For instance:

   "Through this drawing, may I release past burdens and welcome new beginnings." "Let this artwork be a reflection of my inner transformation and growth."

   "As the moon shifts and changes, so too may I embrace the fluidity and evolution within me."

6. **Paper In:** As you state your words, visualize them enveloping the space, creating a sacred circle of intent around you.

7. **Energize Your Materials:** Hold your pencils in between both hands. Imagine golden light from your heart swirling down your arms and into your hands. Infuse your pencils with your intention, imagining them as extensions of your inner self and the moon's energy.

8. **Affirmation of Trust:** Conclude by affirming your trust in the process with words like: "I trust in the journey of creation, guided by the moon's wisdom. May my hand be steady, my vision clear, and my intention manifest through every stroke."

9. **Begin Your Drawing:** With your intention firmly set, you can now start your Lunar Eclipse Drawing ritual, confident that every line, shade, and hue you create is infused with purpose and magic.

As you draw, let the intention simmer in the background of your consciousness, allowing it to subtly guide your hand and decisions, making the artwork a true reflection of both the lunar energies and your personal intentions.

10. **Blessing Once Complete:** As the shadow passes and the moon emerges, signaling the culmination of the eclipse, it's a moment of profound energy—a perfect time to seal your ritual with a heartfelt blessing. You can say your own or here's one:

"Moon above, both shadowed and bright,
Thank you for sharing your beauty tonight.
As this celestial event draws to a close,
I'm grateful for the wonder and the introspection it bestows.

"With every phase, every ebb and flow,
You remind us of life's rhythm, its gentle tempo.
Now, as the night continues its serene glide,
I hold close the feelings and insights you provide.

"May the moments of reflection and calm remain,
Guiding my thoughts, my actions, my aim.
Thank you, moon, for this peaceful night's end,
I cherish the tranquility and the messages you send."

You can then take a few moments to sit in silence, reflecting on the ritual, the energies experienced, and the blessings received. This concluding blessing serves as a bridge, transitioning you from the sacred space of the ritual back into the everyday realm, carrying with you the moon's transformative energy. When ready, place your drawing in a safe space or your sacred space.

Solar Eclipse Ritual

Note: Unlike Lunar Eclipses, Solar Eclipses are quick! They can be as short as ten seconds to as long as just over seven minutes. This Chakra

Alignment Ritual doesn't have to be done at the same time as the Eclipse, however, if you're able to do on the same that would be great! You can also do this any time you want to release and burn away blockages, low vibrations, and when you intuitively sense it's time for a repeat!

Chakra Alignment with the Eclipse

Purpose: This ritual aims to harness the unique energies of the solar eclipse to cleanse, balance, and align the chakras, promoting inner harmony and increasing manifesting vibrations.

MATERIALS:

- A comfortable cushion or mat to sit or lie on.
- Optional: Seven crystals corresponding to each chakra (e.g., Amethyst for Crown, Lapis Lazuli for Third Eye, Aquamarine for Throat, Rose Quartz or Green Aventurine for Heart, Citrine or Sunstone for Solar Plexus, Carnelian for Sacral, and Red Jasper or Garnet for Root).
- Journal and writing tool
- Optional: Background meditation music or nature sounds.

DIRECTIONS:

1. Preparation: Find a quiet, peaceful spot where you won't be disturbed. It doesn't need to have a direct view of the eclipse, but should be somewhere you feel comfortable and safe. Lay your mat or cushion down.

2. Centering: Close your eyes and take deep breaths. Feel yourself becoming present in the moment, releasing any external worries or distractions.

3. Visualize the Eclipse: Imagine the sun and moon above you. Visualize the dance of the moon moving in front of the sun, casting a shadow upon the Earth and, more intimately, upon you.

4. Connect to the Root Chakra:

   - Location: Base of the spine.

   - Visualization: Imagine a spinning red disc or ball of light. As the eclipse progresses, visualize any blockages in this chakra being shadowed and cleansed away.

   - Optional: Place the Red Jasper or Garnet on this spot.

5. Move to the Sacral Chakra:

   - Location: Just below the navel.

   - Visualization: A vibrant orange light. Let the eclipse's energy wash over it, refreshing and revitalizing your creativity and passion.

   - Optional: Place the Carnelian here.

6. Progress to the Solar Plexus Chakra:

   - Location: Upper abdomen.

   - Visualization: A brilliant yellow light. Feel the alignment of this chakra with the celestial bodies, adjusting and amplifying its energy of confidence and courage.

   - Optional: Position the Citrine or Sunstone on this spot.

7. Focus on the Heart Chakra:

   - Location: Center of the chest, just above the heart.

   - Visualization: A radiant green or pink light. Allow feelings of love and compassion to flow as the eclipse's energy purifies this center.

   - Optional: Place the Rose Quartz or Green Aventurine here.

8. Shift to the Throat Chakra:

    - Location: Throat.

    - Visualization: A bright blue light. Let any communication blocks be eclipsed and released.

    - Optional: Set the Aquamarine on this spot.

9. Connect to the Third Eye Chakra:

    - Location: Forehead, between the eyes.

    - Visualization: An indigo light. Allow intuitive insights to flow as the eclipse's transformative energy works its magic.

    - Optional: Place the Lapis Lazuli here.

10. Reach the Crown Chakra:

    - Location: Top of the head.

    - Visualization: A shimmering violet or white light. Feel a strong cosmic connection to the heavens and the Divine as the sun and moon dance above, aligning and energizing this chakra.

    - Optional: Position the Amethyst Quartz on this spot.

11. Completion: Once you've visualized each chakra being cleansed and aligned with the Eclipse's energy, imagine a protective golden light surrounding your entire body. Slowly bring your awareness back to your surroundings. Listen to the sounds around you. Feel the light and warmth of the space. Take a cleansing breath. When you are ready, wiggle and stretch your fingers and your toes. Gently open your eyes.

Sit in silent gratitude for a few moments, thanking the universe for its guidance. Journal any insights you noticed or experienced. If you've used crystals, cleanse them afterward, setting them aside to be charged under the next full moon.

*Under the gaze of
Sirius,
so radiant and true,
may all that you seek
come flowing to you.*

Sirius Gateway

3 JULY - 7 JULY

It's that special time of the year again when Sirius, our sun's wise and dazzling big brother, snuggles close to Earth. Think of Sirius as our spiritual sunshine. Just as our sun pampers us with warmth and strengthens our physical bodies, and the moon soothes and expands our emotions, Sirius sprinkles us with spiritual sparkle!

Welcome to the gateway where FREEDOM and INDEPENDECE ring! Sirius Gateway is a personal invitation from the universe to stride into "you doing you" and open up fresh, exciting paths tailored just for you! It's like hitting the cosmic "reset button" for brand new adventures. Believe in your magic, trust those talents, and step into the spotlight of self-reliance. Why? Because you're a dazzling star ready to shine with fierce and bold independence!

Feeling any manifesting roadblocks? Maybe it's a sneaky fear or trying to please someone else? Maybe it's an ancestorial message of unworthiness? This is the aligned time to dive deep and discover those hidden keys to unlocking *your* freedom!

Not sure? No problem! This gateway occurs under the intuitive sign of Cancer, so expect your inner knowing to be buzzing! Your trusty sixth sense is going to be sending you all kinds of cosmic signals. And while your brain might try to play the "are you sure?" game, remember to let your intuition guide you.

Use this time for manifesting!

1. What do you want brought into your life?

   For example, abundance of love, money health? Fertile ground for pregnancy, creativity, or opportunities? Rebirth in self-confidence, self-care, or in those dreams buried so deep?

2. Based on your answer(s) above, write out each desire in a positive affirmation as if you've already achieved this.

   For example: Let's say you were thinking, I want all of the above, Trish! Great! Then, your affirmation could be, *"I am receiving all that I desire."* Maybe you're in a place where you are desiring peace-of-mind. Your affirmation could be, *"Every day in every way I am healthier, happier, and more confident."*

3. Sirius Gateway is an elevated time to work with spirit helpers.

   Choose one of the 3 spirit guides or all of them!

   1) Call on Angels.

   - Ask your guardian angel for assistance
   - Ask Archangel Barachiel for guidance in success, prosperity and abundance
   - Ask Archangel Jeremial for help being strong and finding the new, positive path

   There are many more angels, if you feel led to call on another, please trust your intuition. Often, my students in my Angels On Demand course, comment they begin working with their guardian angel and soon an archangel name pops into their mind, only to discover that is the perfect archangel to call on! Angels love working with you, so invite them!

When communicating with angels, talk to them just like you're speaking with a dear family member. They already intimately know you and love you. They know your heart and your intention, so remove any worries. And, there is no need to be formal with words like "thou" or whatever you're thinking sounds ancient and angelic. Just be you. Keep it simple. Say something like, "Archangel Barachiel, please help me." You've got this!

2) **Call on Fairies.**

- Talk to Daisy Fairies for easy communication and a positive outcome
- Talk to Light Fairy to illuminate the best path to manifest faster and best outcome
- Talk to Lavender Fairy for total peace and quick healing

Call on fairies to help align with Sirius Gateway's elevated energy and vibrations. When communicating with fairies, speak aloud in nature. Trust your intuition for their replies. You may sense a message or experience a feeling of joy. Fairies are communicating!

3) **Call on the Goddess of Sirius, Goddess Sopdet.**

- When manifesting new starts, new beginnings and new light to shine on your dreams
- When you need increased productivity or growth
- When you need help releasing and trusting the outcome

Goddess Sopdet is the brightest star in the Canis Major constellation. She signaled the start of the Ancient Egyptian New Year and is a symbol of fertility. When communicating with her, go outside under each night sky. Try to find her star. It's okay if it's cloudy or you don't have time to locate her. Speak aloud and make your request known. Close your eyes and imagine her loving light shimmering down upon you. Be patient and open to any intuitive messages you sense. Trust you are receiving her guidance. Thank her for her messages, encouragement, and assistance.

You can continue working with Goddess Sopdet even after this gateway.

4) Each day apply your manifesting checklist.

Morning:

- Imagine your successful day prior to getting out of bed.
- State your affirmation 3 times and every time you pass a mirror.
- Stay alert to the spiritual messages provided throughout the day.
- Take action.

Evening:

- Write 3 things you noticed during the day.
- Write 3 things you're grateful for.
- Spend 7 minutes visualizing and feeling the joy of having already accomplished your dreams.

This manifesting daily habit can continue throughout the year!

Journal insights and manifesting wins. Even if you're manifesting stronger intuition, this is something to celebrate! You are claiming your soul's independence and the freedom to achieve the life you desire.

"I am free to attract and receive all good things."

Lionsgate Gateway

28 JULY - 12 AUGUST

The Lionsgate Gateway is like our universe's annual celestial party, kicking off on the 28th of July and dancing its way through till the 12th of August. The peak? That's right on 8/8, a portal date that's not just cool because of the symmetry but also packed with manifesting significance in both numerology and astrology.

Have you ever tipped the number 8 on its side? It transforms into the infinity sign, symbolizing a beautiful balance between our tangible and intangible worlds. Plus, this wonderful, dynamic number 8 is like a super strong magnet for abundance and prosperity. Cha-ching, baby!

Now, let's talk zodiac vibes. The Lionsgate Gateway happens right in the heart of Leo season. Leo's energy is all about channeling that fierce, feminine flair, sprinkling creativity, nurturing, and deep intuition into our lives. Think of it as getting a dose of lioness courage to chase after your dreams, while also learning the graceful dance of patience, balance, and a touch of irresistible charm.

And here's the most magical part: throughout this gateway, the universe will send you little (or maybe big!) vibrational gifts, upgrades, and boosts. From vivid dreams to gut feelings to unexpected signs, it's all the universe's way of nudging you forward. Trust in these signs—they're not just random happenings but intentional cosmic winks meant to inspire and encourage you.

Use this 8/8 for manifesting!

1. **Set your intention.**

   I know you've read this repeatedly, but by setting your intention, the universe opens and connects you with endless possibilities to support your intention.

   I usually set this intention, *"It is my intention to soak up the energy boost of Lionsgate Portal to use as I desire throughout the rest of the year."*

   (If you aren't sure what intentions to set, you can grab my intention setting worksheet here at www.shineandalignwithtrish.com/intentionsettingworksheet)

2. **Sit in the Sun.**

   Go outdoors and sit in the sunlight absorbing this transformative manifesting energy. You can apply sunscreen, wear a hat, or just be in the sun. Soak up the manifesting sun's magic for 8 minutes. Be confident that as you bask in the sun you ARE disintegrating the blockages and receiving and attuning to the higher manifesting and spiritual frequency. You can enjoy the energy in quiet or add a meditation like my Lionsgate Portal Meditation on YouTube.

3. **If need be, you can continue this step in the shade.**

   Now that you're feeling supercharged, and maybe a little sleepy, it's time to write.

   In your journal, write what you intend on manifesting. This is a great opportunity to stretch yourself. Dream bigger!

This is the time to explore manifesting:

- Miracles
- Accepting your gifts
- Overcoming hurt
- Attracting the love of your life
- Creating an app
- Writing a book
- Releasing anything blocking your peace
- Stepping into your power
- Being heard
- Feeling and knowing you're desirable
- Anything your intuition is sharing

Complete this sentence in your journal. "It is my intention to manifest…" Add as many as you'd like beginning each sentence this way.

4. **Look over your sentences and read each one aloud, changing the words from, "It is my intention to…" to "I am a manifesting magnet for…"**

For example, *"It is my intention to manifest being a successful speaker at a TED talk"* becomes, *"I am a manifesting magnet for being a successful speaker at a TED talk."*

Read these new sentences aloud. Use your strong voice. Roar like the lion. As you're speaking these, feel the truth of your statement vibrating throughout your entire being while imagining it has already happened. When you've finished with your list, conclude with, *"I align with the confidence and courage to receive these or something better."*

5. **Time to daydream or take a catnap!** Spend another 8 minutes daydreaming that these have manifested. Give each sentence its due attention. This is a precious time as you are working alongside the magic of the Lionsgate Portal, Sirius, Goddess Sopdet and your guardian angel. You are loved and meant to have your dreams come true.

"I accept that I am powerful."

Merkaba Portal

12 DECEMBER - WINTER SOLSTICE

Winter Solstice occurs any time from 20 December to 23 December

Every December brings a touch of magic with it. From the 12th right up to the Winter Solstice, the universe treats us to a special gift. Think of it as a celestial tune-up! Whether we're aware of it or not, our spirits are given a little boost, infused with healing vibes, more distinct angel whispers, and an amplified vibrational hum. Embracing the beauty and might of this portal is like opening a door to a more profound love and a more radiant inner glow. So, welcome this time with open arms and hearts, ready to shine even brighter!

Merkaba is an ancient Hebrew word that's actually a compilation of three separate words.

>   *Mer - Light*
>   *Ka - Spirit*
>   *Ba - Body*

Your Merkaba field extends beyond your aura field. This is where your soul's destiny blueprint resides. This is where you have a clearer, greater, and easier connection with the Divine. Tapping into this sacred space not only deepens your spiritual journey but also aligns you with your true purpose. By understanding and embracing the potential of your Merkaba field, you open the door to divine guidance, ensuring every step you take is in harmony with the universe's prosperous design for you. Embrace this connection and it will illuminate your path forward.

What upgrade would you like?

Clearer intuition? Healing? Peace? Confidence in your manifesting? Quicker manifesting connection? Stronger angel connection? Even if you're unsure, connect with this gateway portal.

How to Use the Merkaba Portal

1. Know what you want to manifest.

2. Set your timer for 12 minutes.

3. Get comfortable and close your eyes. Imagine yourself in the center of the Star of David, also known as a 6-pointed star or star tetrahedron.

4. Imagine yourself sitting or standing as you visualize golden flecks of light swirling around you. Each is filled with energy, love, and a divine connection.

5. Imagine the lights suddenly amplifying and sparkling signaling Archangel Metatron is approaching. Breathe in this divine connection. Archangel Metatron asks, "What would you like to manifest?"

6. Answer from your heart. You don't have to speak this aloud. Just mentally share your response.

7. Imagine Archangel Metatron asking, "Would you like my assistance?"

8. If you answer yes, then notice any intuitive insights. Trust the messages flowing to you through each of your five senses and your feelings and knowing.

9. Imagine your dream has manifested. Lean into that completion, experiencing the joy and gratitude.

10. With every inhale imagine energy streaming in, beginning below the soles of your feet, swirling up through your body to the top of your head. This vibrant, loving energy traveling through and around your body.

11. With every exhale, imagine all energetic blockages recognized, releasing, and disintegrating.

12. When the timer sounds, thank Archangel Metatron. Take a cleansing breath and open your eyes.

You may want to sip on water afterward.

Take a moment to jot down any thoughts, visions, or feelings that pop up during your meditation. Remember, there's no detail too small! If you make it a daily habit, have a little chat with Archangel Metatron and the angels, asking them for some extra wisdom. And always, always give a hearty thanks for their gentle guidance and loving presence in your journey. Happy journaling!

Manifesting Tips

If possible, do this exercise each day of the portal. If you can only do once then make sure you do this on 12/12.

Amplify the energy by performing this at 12:12 am or pm or both.

Stay observant for signs, symbols, and messages from your angels!

"I am a divine manifesting magnet."

ONLY POSITIVE ENERGY

Retrogrades

Retrogrades, particularly the well-known Mercury retrograde, are periods when celestial bodies appear to move backward in their orbit, as observed from Earth. While retrogrades often get a bad rap for causing confusion, miscommunication, or mishaps, they can also be a potent time for reflection, introspection, and reassessment.

Retrogrades are powerful periods to reassess and refine your intentions. Consider the root word, "retro," meaning "backward," and you have the energy for this phase. It's like jumping into the DeLorean with Marty from the movie *Back to the Future* and rewatching all of your previous manifesting successes and wins.

- Revisit times you succeeded.
- Remember your dreams.
- Reminisce about things you did that kept your energy elevated, optimistic, and encouraged.

Consider retrogrades a gentle nudge to dive deep into the realm of "re's": Recall, Reinforce, Reflect, Remember, and Reimagine. As you journey back in time, sifting through your past experiences, ask yourself: What pearls of wisdom can you gather? How can those insights shape your manifesting journey today? By embracing the lessons of yesterday, you're setting the stage for a brighter, clearer tomorrow. Buckle up and get ready to time travel backward and then blasting your manifesting success forward!

Each planet offers distinct lessons and insights. During its retrograde phase, it beckons us to reflect on its specific domain. Consider Mercury, the messenger planet, known for governing communication. When it treads backward, it's an opportune moment to journey inward. Reflect on past manifestations: What were the words you whispered to yourself, shared with others, and sent out to the cosmos? By revisiting those potent affirmations, you not only rekindle the magic of bygone successes but also pave the way to approach future manifestations with renewed clarity and intent.

Manifesting with each retrograde and its planet is included in the *Planet* chapter.

Here's a general Retrograde ritual designed to help you navigate any retrograde period with grace and mindfulness:

Retrograde Reflection Ritual

Purpose: This ritual aids in grounding, clarity, and protection during a retrograde. It also promotes self-reflection and understanding, helping you to internalize the lessons this cosmic event offers.

MATERIALS:

- A candle (preferably silver or white)
- A piece of paper and a pen
- Incense or sage (for cleansing)
- A small bowl of water (representing emotional clarity)
- A crystal (clear quartz for clarity, amethyst for calm, or black tourmaline for protection)

DIRECTIONS:

1. Preparation: Find a quiet space where you won't be disturbed. Cleanse the area by lighting the incense or sage, letting the smoke purify your surroundings and creating a sacred space.

2. Lighting the Candle: As you light the candle, set your intention: *"May this light guide and protect me during this retrograde, illuminating my path with clarity and understanding."*

3. Grounding: Close your eyes and take deep breaths. Visualize roots growing from your body, anchoring you deep into the Earth, grounding you in the present moment.

4. Reflection & Release:

   - On the piece of paper, write down any challenges, misunderstandings, or negative patterns you've noticed during the retrograde.

   - Reflect on each point. Is there a lesson? Is there something you need to reassess or approach differently?

   - Once you've reflected, say out loud, *"I acknowledge these challenges and release them. I am open to the lessons and growth they bring."*

   - Safely burn the paper in the candle flame (or tear it up), symbolizing release and transformation.

5. Affirmation & Intention Setting:

   - Holding the crystal in your hand, set an intention for the remainder of the retrograde. It could be something like, *"I navigate this period with grace, understanding, and patience,"* or *"I am protected and guided during this time of reflection."*

   - As you set your intention, visualize it being absorbed by the crystal. Keep this crystal with you during the retrograde as a talisman of your intention.

6. Water Meditation:
   - Gaze into the bowl of water, using it as a tool for meditation and clarity.
   - Ask the universe or your higher self for guidance on any decisions you're contemplating or for clarity on any confusions you're facing. Allow insights to come to you, even if they're subtle.

7. Closing:
   - Express gratitude: *"Thank you, universe, for the lessons and insights of this retrograde. I am prepared, protected, and aligned with my highest good."*
   - Extinguish the candle, knowing its energy will continue to work with you.
   - Store the crystal in a safe place, and pour the water outside, returning it to nature.

Remember, while retrogrades can be challenging, they're also an opportunity for growth and self-discovery. This ritual can be tailored to your personal beliefs and can be done at the beginning, middle, or even the end of a retrograde period.

"I am able to make the most of the universe rewinding, realigning, and renewing my manifesting mojo!"

Manifesting
with the
Planets

✴

*Every planet carries its own distinct energy and message.
Whether a planet dominates your sign, sits prominently,
or takes a retrograde spin, it offers valuable insights to
enhance your manifesting journey. Delve deeper and
harness the wisdom these celestial bodies bestow.*

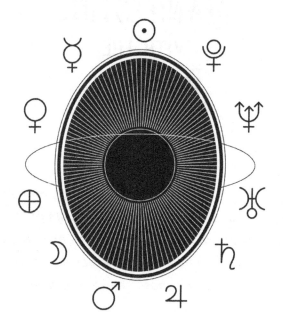

Meanings & Their Path

Imagine planets as our cosmically cool relatives—those older, wiser family members with stories that can make your jaw drop. They've danced through the galaxy, experienced celestial dramas, and gathered cosmic wisdom.

Dive into this chapter as if you're reuniting at a grand family gathering. Each planet, with its unique personality and flair, has some nuggets of wisdom to share. And when you really listen, they can unveil shortcuts to your manifesting dreams.

We'll be chatting with all nine celestial members (and yes, that includes Pluto—once family, always family!). No need for an astrological degree here. By the end of this section, you'll have a friendly rapport with each planet, understanding their guiding influences and pinpointing the exact cosmic vibes to amplify your manifesting mojo.

A planet's movement is good to know and is marked in the *Monthly Manifesting Pages*.

- *Direct* is when the planet is moving and grooving on its normal path in front of Earth. *Direct* is a manifesting time of forward momentum. Take action. This is when the planet is offering to hold our hands and guide us. Weeee!

- *Retrograde* is when the planet seems to be going backward from our point of view on Earth. *Retrograde* is a time of slowing down. Breathe. Remembering your awesomeness from the past. Revisit and review past experiences in the areas of the planet's expertise – and apply to current manifesting needs. You don't have to remember this. This is spelled out for you each month.

- *Pre-shadow* (leading up to the change in direction from direct to retrograde) and *post-shadow* days (days following exiting the retrograde phase). While both periods showcase the energy, pre-shadow is the retrograde energy increasing and post-shadow is the retrograde energy decreasing.

Connect With Your Planet

Picture this: when a planet rules your astrological sign, it's like you've won the cosmic VIP pass. You're their star pupil, their favorite person in the cosmic dance! They roll out the celestial red carpet just for you, ensuring you're always in sync. This connection is intuitive, like a silent whisper or a secret nudge only you can perceive. Don't worry, I'm not asking you to add 'Talk to planets' to your ever-growing to-do list. Just be open-hearted, tune into those subtle vibes, and occasionally, take a moment to check in: 'Hey, what's my guiding planet trying to tell me?' I know, it might sound a tad out there. But trust me, as a Gemini with Mercury as my main man, I've felt his gentle guidance. He's whispered the perfect words into my ear, given me timely travel tips, and ensured I never miss a beat. Just like Mercury has my back, your ruling planet is ready to be your cosmic BFF too!

When connecting with a planet, whether yours or not, there are some simple ways to energetically connect.

1. Listen to the sound of the planet. There are recordings of the sounds from outer space. You can find this on YouTube or on my YouTube playlist entitled, "Planets." Venus is one of my favorites!

2. Connect with the color of your ruling planet. Find or make a candle in the planet's color.

Sun – orange | Leo

Moon – black and white | Cancer

Mercury – gray | Gemini and Virgo

Venus – gray-blue | Taurus and Libra

Mars – reddish-brown | Aries and Scorpio

Jupiter – orange-white | Sagittarius and Pisces

Saturn – pale gold | Capricorn and Aquarius

Uranus – aquamarine | Aquarius

Neptune – dark blue | Pisces

Pluto – brown and cream | Scorpio

Chiron – gray | Ophiuchus

State your intention, *"I am connecting with the planet* _____ *(fill in the blank)."* Light your candle. Take a cleansing breath. Feel the connection. Keep your candle lit as long as you'd like. Before you extinguish the flame, thank the planet. This gratitude is a vibration and is felt by the universe.

3. Dedicate a crystal to be your planet's connection. This is *your* choice. You may intuitively feel a particular crystal, like tektite or meteorite. Trust your intuition. Opals were discovered on Mars by the Mars Rover, so choose the crystal that you *feel* it is your link to your planet.

Sun – amber, sunstone

Moon – moonstone, pearl

Mercury – emerald, chrysoprase

Venus – kunzite, rose quartz

Mars – carnelian

Jupiter – amethyst

Saturn – chalcedony

Uranus – labradorite

Neptune – lapis lazuli

Pluto – obsidian

Chiron – malachite

Once you've chosen your crystal, hold it in both hands. Close your eyes and feel yourself opening to a deeper connection with the crystal and its tie to your planet. When you feel a bond has been created, thank the crystal and open your eyes. Slip the crystal in your pocket, place it in your sacred space or by your bed. You can choose to include the crystal in meditations or just connect while sleeping.

Now, time for the family reunion with the planets!

SUN

Sun

Sun, friendly, loving and original head of the family.
He loves you and fuels your manifesting fires.

QUIRKS: Sun is like the radiant, loyal, devoted dad of the family tree.

SPECIALTIES: Optimism. Vitality. Encouraging. Success.

FAVORITE SIGN: Leo

ADVICE: "Shine your unique light and manifest."

The sun is the divine masculine energy. He cheers you on. He knows you are equipped and able. The sun provides the fiery energy, fuels your confidence and the focus to manifest.

Your sun sign attributes are the strengths and the chinks in your personality. This driving force sets you up to manifest – success or failure. So, every time you look at the sun, remember to keep your focus on manifesting the outcome you desire. Just like the sunflower growing into a vibrant display of beauty, it starts with a seed. And, so does manifesting. Plant your seed in the fertile ground of your soul. Nurture with your focused intentional thoughts and mindset. And allow the sun to shine on your dreams.

The sun reminds you to celebrate you. Your personality and its strengths are part of your divine purpose. Your gifts stem from your awareness of your beautiful personality and the part it plays in your manifesting.

One of my favorite Aesop Fables is *The North Wind and the Sun*. The North Wind and the Sun are having a chat regarding who's stronger and spot a man in a coat along the road. A deal is struck that whoever gets the man to remove his coat is declared the stronger. The wind blows and blows, of course, the man clenches his coat tighter. The sun shines and shines, and gently warming the man, he eagerly removes his coat.

Manifesting with the sun is like that. No need to force. Stay positive. Shine and allow.

Work with the Sun when you want:

- Growth
- Abundance
- Focus
- Energy
- Confidence
- Acceptance
- Creativity

Sunshine for Manifesting

- Identify the sun's current sign and the qualities it offers. Apply the beneficial attributes to your manifesting plan.

- Get outdoors. Get in the sunshine. Soak up the Vitamin D and all the benefits. Imagine the sun warming your dreams and the fertile manifesting ground.

- Every time you look at the sun, remember to keep your focus on manifesting the outcome you desire. Take a cleansing breath. In your mind's eye imagine all has manifested exactly as you desired. Imagine the sun continually to shine on your happily ever after.

MOON

Moon

Moon, inspiring, loving and compassionate ancient family.
She loves you and nurtures your soul, your dreams and deepest desires.

QUIRKS: Moon is like the quiet, nurturing and understanding,
devoted mom of the family tree.

SPECIALTIES: Emotions. Nurturing. Intuitive. Cycles.

FAVORITE SIGN: Cancer

ADVICE: "Align your emotions. Trust your intuition.
And, accept the fact that you are a divine magical being
already aligned with the manifesting flow."

The moon is the divine feminine energy. She goes deep. She reaches out to you every night. She knows by nurturing your soul and cocooning yourself in love, you emotionally open to receiving the bounty life has to offer. Whatever the deepest desires you truly want to manifest, the Moon wants to assist.

Moon communicates through emotions and intuition. How you're feeling and responding is telling you if you're truly aligned with receiving what you want to manifest or if you've got some blockages.

Your intuition is the right path to manifest. Tune her out, and you risk incurring manifesting delays.

Work with Moon when you want to manifest in the areas of:

- Family and home
- Healing and understanding
- Spiritual work
- Fertility
- Aligning emotions with manifesting
- Heightened intuitive work

The moon is associated with goddesses throughout time and cultures. She represents the phases of our life. She brings light, inspiration and love. Wherever you are in your manifesting cycle, the moon will embrace, encourage, and empower you. Explore the *Moon* chapter for deepening your moon connection and creating a plan to manifest with the moon's natural cycle.

By aligning with her rhythms, you are not just wishing upon the stars but actively harnessing a cosmic force to bring your deepest desires to fruition. As you move forward, remember that each lunar phase offers a unique opportunity for reflection and growth. Allow the moon's gentle illumination to guide your path, and let her transformative energy amplify your manifesting prowess. In doing so, you not only honor the celestial dance but also deepen your connection to the universe's abundant gifts. Embrace the moon, trust your intuition, and watch as your dreams gracefully unfold.

The moon's gentle pull not only moves the tides but the currents of our innermost dreams.

MERCURY

Mercury

*Mercury, chatty and sometimes obnoxious, is still your
wise, albeit, snarky ancient nephew. He loves you and will
give your manifesting dreams wings to take flight.*

QUIRKS: Mercury is the excited, energetic and chatty nephew.

SPECIALTIES: Communication. Contracts. Travel. Electronics.

FAVORITE SIGNS: Gemini and Virgo

ADVICE: "Clear up your affirmations and you'll clear your
path to speedy manifesting of your dreams."

Mercury is closest to the Sun. He zips around, cheering us on and inspiring action. Mercury provides the extra energy and warmth when we hit a wall, need clarity or creative inspiration.

Work with Mercury when you want:

Knowledge about going forward. For example, if you want to manifest a new car, Mercury guides you to the vehicle pros and cons and even will reveal a better deal.

Communication — hearing and sharing your intuition, communicating with others, communicating with angels or spirit guides, speaking, writing, and networking.

- Create your affirmations for manifesting
- Communicate your dreams with others
- Reconnect with youthful energy and belief

When Mercury is Retrograde

It can seem like Mercury is always retrograding. That's because he does three to four times a year. Given the not-so-loving nickname, "The Trickster," when retrograde, Mercury messes up our phones, computers, cars, travel plans and creates this intense desire to hook back up with an ex. However, Mercury Retrograde doesn't have to be a bad time. In fact, Mercury Retrograde provides opportunities if you'll pause and take advantage of it!

Navigating Mercury Retrograde

- Give yourself extra time with any appointments or necessary travel
- Review texts, emails and calendar days and times
- Think. And think again before you speak
- Use this as an opportunity to stay in a positive mindset, no matter the circumstances.
- Slip a crystal into your pocket for additional protection.

    Here are my go-to crystals:

    > **Black Tourmaline:** The ultimate cosmic bouncer! Keeps those retrograde vibes at bay and ensures you're surfing the wave, not drowning in it.

> **Blue Lace Agate:** Your zen master in crystal form. When Mercury Retro gets sassy, this one keeps things chill.

> **Rose Quartz:** The universal BFF, mending bridges and sending love beam signals. Making sure you're feeling the love, 24/7.

Mercury Retrograde for Manifesting

Remember a time from the past when your dream came true. Think back and reminisce of what you thought and said. Reconnect to the excitement and gratitude of the successful journey, even the bumps encountered along the way.

Don't get frustrated when any glitches occur. Immediately explore if a new door is opening. Perhaps a door that had been opened in the past and since forgotten.

This retrograde may be just the one to help you manifest what you want!

Gemini and Virgo, you'll be impacted more than other signs. Mercury Retrograde will lend its curiosity to explore more of the out-of-the-box thinking and dreams. You'll also be able to see the pros and cons of manifesting your dream. Use this time to talk yourself into pursuing your dreams.

VENUS

Venus

Venus, elegant and feminine, is your nurturing, albeit, sexy ancient auntie. She loves you and will provide your manifesting with the love and kindness it needs to succeed.

QUIRKS: Venus is the gorgeous, confident and elegant auntie.

SPECIALTIES: Beauty, Arts. Money. Love.

FAVORITE SIGNS: Taurus and Libra

ADVICE: "Embrace love in all things and you will be a magnet for manifesting your dreams."

Venus is often seen in our sky and felt in our hearts. She calls out to us in the allure of a song, elegance in art, and the magnificence of mother nature. She encourages us to celebrate our own unique gifts and beauty. Venus provides the extra confidence when we're ready to take a risk, put our hearts out there or need to love and accept ourselves again.

Work with Venus when you want:

To attract beauty, wealth and love. For example, if you want to manifest a better relationship, Venus guides you to the steps to take beginning with loving yourself. By doing this, you're communicating to the universe that you are worthy, deserving and ready to receive what you want to manifest.

Cooperation — getting support from those around, including your boss and co-workers, family members, and friends.

- Create your vision board for manifesting
- Decorate your bedroom, sacred space, home or office
- Dream and align with your dream having already come true
- Open the energy of balance and harmony in your life
- Reconnect with your soul's passion
- Reveal your soul's passion

When Venus is Retrograde

Venus can throw our love life and finances into havoc. Harmony on the home front may be challenged. Ex-lovers may try to connect. Credit cards and online banking may go on the fritz. This is the time to sit and be beautiful.

Venus Retrograde is always offering love and support.

Navigate Venus Retrograde

- Do NOT try a new haircut, makeup regimen or major beauty shift
- Do make extra time for delving into self-care and self-love
- Splurge on enjoying the luxury already in your life

Venus Retrograde for Manifesting

Remember a time when you felt prosperous or really loved. Go all in exploring this memory lane. Connect with every emotion. Recall the joy, appreciation and magic through each of your senses. To anchor this energy, draw an abstract that captures the beauty, love and gratitude.

This retrograde may be just the one to help you manifest what you want!

Taurus and Libra you'll be impacted more than other signs. Venus Retrograde will lovingly show you where you may be out-of-balance. She'll ask you to remember you are worthy and deserving of love and your dreams.

MARS

Mars

*Mars, courageous and sometimes arrogant, is still your
strong, assertive ancient cousin. He loves you and will push
your dream from beginning to champion status.*

QUIRKS: Mars is like the confident, get-it-done, jock cousin.

SPECIALTIES: Strength. Courage. Competitive. Physical.

FAVORITE SIGNS: Aries and Scorpio

ADVICE: "Take action! Do one thing each day and you will
be on the victorious side of manifesting your dreams."

Mars is like the athletic young jock whose energy is contagious. He knows how to win and sweeps you into the enthusiastic confidence. Mars provides the tenacity to help you get up when feeling discouraged, have the determination to pursue a new dream or the intestinal fortitude during any opposition.

Work with Mars when you want:

Fearlessness to pursue your dreams. Energy, courage and confidence to overcome any obstacle. Training necessary to achieve our goal.

- Create a plan of action to manifest your dreams
- Put blinders on and listen to the confidence and encouragement of your soul
- Reconnect with inner and outer strength

When Mars is Retrograde

Forget arguing about what's fair and what isn't. Sex may seem off. Things can seem like stumbling into a brick wall. This is a perfect time to go within. Where are you doubting yourself? What are you truly communicating to yourself? Do you honestly know you are a winner? Deserving? If not, this retrograde is the perfect time to sniff out the blockages and open to your strengths. Exit this retrograde knowing you are a champion!

Navigate Mars Retrograde

- Explore new workout programs
- Look in the mirror and give yourself pep talks
- Avoid arguments

Mars Retrograde for Manifesting

Get moving! Go for a walk, run, or stretch. While you are moving, state your affirmations out loud. *"I am confident in pursuing and achieving my dreams! I have manifested my dreams!"* You are calling in the dream manifested as you are taking the steps. Your whole mind, body and spirit is engaged.

This can be a time of interference and glitches. People may be cranky or increasingly negative about your dreams. Do not give any energy to entertaining those distractions. Stay focused. Concentrate on your win.

This retrograde may be just the one to help you manifest what you want!

Aries and Scorpio, you'll be impacted more than other signs. Mars Retrograde will lends its power to discovering beneficial detours and new action steps. You'll also be able to see where you have succeeded before and the knowingness that you will succeed again! Use this time to pump yourself up and know you are achieving your dreams.

JUPITER

Jupiter

*Jupiter, big, bold, and sometimes honest to a fault is still a
kind and helpful ancient uncle. He loves you and will reward
your faith and optimism that dreams do come true.*

QUIRKS: Jupiter is like the friendly, enthusiastic and rich uncle.

SPECIALTIES: Adventure. Good Luck. Opportunities. Electronics.

FAVORITE SIGNS: Sagittarius and Pisces

ADVICE: "Be open to the generosity of the universe.
Once you do, prosperity showers upon you!"

Often identified as the "Daddy Warbucks" of the planets, Jupiter offers his wallet open to you. What do you need? I'm gonna help! Jupiter doesn't just give the financial assist. It's the good luck, new ideas, and opportunities. Jupiter has the attitude and belief that 'of course the dream has manifested!'

Work with Jupiter when you want:

To manifest! Jupiter knows how to find the shower of blessings.

Need to take a risk. Jupiter will help you shine and thrive.

Working with Jupiter leads to expansion and growth within your life – spiritually, mentally and physically. You'll boldly find yourself changed for the better.

- Fearlessness to seize the moment, opportunity and good fortune
- Explore new areas of wisdom to achieve your dreams
- Be open to new and easier ways of receiving good luck

When Jupiter is Retrograde

Overdoing it? Places of excess? Areas where you focus on the half-empty. This teaching and wise planet will lovingly reveal places where change must occur.

Navigate Jupiter Retrograde

- Set better and clearer boundaries
- Trust your inner knowingness for the answers
- Let go of the things, thoughts, and beliefs that restrict your joy, love, and success

Jupiter Retrograde for Manifesting

Go all out on positive affirmations. Splurge! Jupiter has the insider knowledge to the right path to manifest easier and faster. So focus your energy and attention on this.

Practice daily gratitude. Maybe you're already writing in a gratitude journal, but if you'll increase your gratitude, you will increase your manifesting magnetism.

This retrograde may be just the one to help you manifest what you want!

Sagittarius and Pisces you'll be impacted more than other signs. Jupiter Retrograde will lends its loving approach to search your self-expression. By being generous, you receive generosity. By being kind, you receive kindness. By being loving, you receive love. This retrograde offers a chance to boost your vibration and align with higher frequencies of love and abundance.

SATURN

Saturn

Saturn, strict, serious and rather old-school-rigid-teacher, is still your brilliant and mature ancient uncle. He loves you and will provide the plan, steps and priorities and if you'll do the work you'll find your dreams manifested easier and faster.

QUIRKS: Saturn is like the strict, no fun and boring uncle.

SPECIALTIES: Commitment. Structure. Rules. Teacher.

FAVORITE SIGNS: Capricorn and Aquarius

ADVICE: "Use your time wisely and you'll manifest your dreams."

Saturn use to be considered the edge of the universe. He embodied the phrase, "the buck stops here," meaning he was the gatekeeper, the ruler and enforcer of hard work. No skimping. Just do it.

Work with Saturn when you want:

Structure. Whether building a home, writing a book or laying out ingredients for a recipe, structure makes the process easier. That's what Saturn reveals. The best structure for the best end result.

- Take responsibility for your dreams manifesting
- Overcoming procrastination
- Prioritizing and scheduling so your life has balance and dreams have room to come true

When Saturn is Retrograde

He's reminding you that you matter. Your opinions, beliefs and goals matter. Stay realistic. Do not set yourself up for failure. Retrograde will help you see where you are trying to squeeze thirty hours of work into a twenty-four hour day. Use this time to strike a sensible and healthy balance.

Navigate Saturn Retrograde

- Identify areas needing closure and shut that door so you can open to the success
- Take an honest look at where you seem blocked from progress and make the necessary changes
- Make a list of priorities, put blinders on and set timers to complete your list

Saturn Retrograde for Manifesting

Is there a mentor who has achieved what you want? Whether you know this person or not, look to see the system they had in place. What steps did they take? What boundaries, schedules, disciplines did they use? Create a framework that will work for you. No rush. Do the research. Do the work. Create your personalized design. Saturn will reward your hard work when he goes direct.

This retrograde may be just the one to help you manifest what you want!

Capricorn and Aquarius, you'll be impacted more than other signs. Saturn Retrograde will provide a realistic view of your energy and where you're giving it. Are you giving too much to others and it's taking away energy and focus from your dreams? Set clear and realistic boundaries. Remember, every time you say "yes" to someone else, you are saying "no" to you. Trust the process. Stay balanced and know that you are worthy of wonderful opportunities.

URANUS

Uranus

*Uranus, cool, unconventional and sometimes peculiar, is still
your brilliant ancient uncle. He loves you and will provide
a radical, fresh, genius new take on manifesting.*

QUIRKS: Uranus is like the innovative, eccentric and rebellious uncle.

SPECIALTIES: Technology. Inventions. Rational Thinking. Electronics.

FAVORITE SIGNS: Aquarius

ADVICE: "Expect the unexpected and you'll discover manifesting
your dreams in ways you didn't know possible."

Uranus is unique, original and extremely comfortable in his own way of doing things. He is the only planet that spins horizontally rather than vertically. I always envisioned Uranus as the Steve Jobs, co-founder of Apple, of the solar system. He brings sudden change with his new ideas and technological advances.

Work with Uranus when you want:

A new, radical approach for an area in your life. Maybe it's time to shake things up. Branch out into the unknown. Maybe it's time to escape into deeper meditation or exploring new elements of your spirituality.

- Being comfortable being uniquely you
- Logic and reasoning to be the guiding force
- Major modifications in your life

When Uranus is Retrograde

Uranus shakes things up creating turmoil and sudden change. As you're sorting through the aftermath, Uranus seems to be saying, "Here you go. Deal with it. You're welcome." It can seem like a pile of chaos, but when the topsy-turviness settles, you'll discover a hidden gem.

Uranus Retrograde doesn't have to be rife with disappointments.

Navigate Uranus Retrograde

- Discover areas of your life that need some liberating or transformation
- Explore online courses, lectures, and new audiobooks
- Celebrate your own quirks, preferences, and unique personality

Uranus Retrograde for Manifesting

Are there areas in your life needing fresh energy and new ideas? Maybe you've become too logical and are thinking, *"It has to manifest this way."* Uranus Retrograde is the perfect time to recall a time you've gone out of your comfort zone and succeeded. Invite discomfort in and let the success begin!

Uranus Retrograding is an opportune time to try that new way of doing something. Get out of the rut and explore. Uranus really does bring breakthroughs in areas that have been stymied. Retrograde will help you see what areas of your life need a shakeup and the new ways to achieve this.

This retrograde may be just the one to help you manifest what you want!

Aquarius, you'll be impacted more than any other sign. Uranus Retrograde will have you reaching out to heal the world. You'll see where your dreams will make the world a better place. By investing in spiritual endeavors like meditation, yoga or other creating healing mandalas you'll receive new insight into manifesting your dreams.

NEPTUNE

Neptune

Neptune, mystical and magical, is still your transforming ancient uncle. He loves you and will empower your spiritual gifts so you can make manifesting magic.

QUIRKS: Neptune is like the handsome, mysterious and romantic uncle.

SPECIALTIES: Imagination. Dreams. Spiritualism. Compassion.

FAVORITE SIGNS: Pisces

ADVICE: "Go deep into your divine self. Accept your creative and magical powers and you will flow in the ever-present manifesting current."

Neptune known as "God of the Sea" swims besides you as you plunge into the deep waters of your soul. He carries a triton that looks like a tuning fork, enabling you to tune into your dreams and the smoothest way to manifest them. Look for his influence and encouragement through music!

Work with Neptune when you want:

Inspiration! Maybe you long for your muse to whisper, encourage, and arouse the passion within. Neptune aligns with change in your life without extreme waves. Neptune ushers in shifts with ease and subtly. This includes healing, artistic expression and nurturing your soul.

- Deepen your spiritual gifts, especially intuition and sensitivities to the spirit world
- Increase compassion in your life with others and yourself
- Ease in expressing yourself

When Neptune is Retrograde

It's a time to go deeper and move beyond any illusions. Where are you kidding yourself? You'll be able to identify and see the realities of situations and relationships. You'll also be able to see where you're romanticizing and ignoring the reality of a situation. Neptune Retrograde will show you where you are sacrificing yourself and it's taking a toll on you physically, spiritually, and mentally. Once he's ripped off the rose-colored glasses you'll be able to make swift changes so you can swim in the deep manifesting waters.

Navigate Neptune Retrograde

- Open to releasing the old and welcoming in the new in a smooth, fluid
- Schedule in spa days, self-care and spiritual retreats
- Keep a dream journal

Neptune Retrograde for Manifesting

What spiritual or new age topic have you wanted to explore? This is the time to fully engage. Pay attention to your intuition as you seek answers through your spiritual pursuits. Maybe you suddenly want to explore becoming a Reiki Master or investing in working with crystals. Divine guidance will be provided. Be open to the known and unknown. Trust your sixth sense!

This retrograde may be just the one to help you manifest what you want!

Pisces, you'll be impacted more than any other sign. Neptune Retrograde will offer clarity as to who you are and why your dreams matter. You'll gain confidence as this timing rips the bandages off and reveals where you may be stuck. You'll identify the situations, people or even your thoughts that have been holding you back from achieving your success. In Retrograde, the murky fog is lifted. The path is cleared. You will be able to see and know what to do to confidently manifest your dreams.

PLUTO

Pluto

Pluto, mysterious and intense, is still your powerful ancient cousin. He loves you and will assist in taking your dreams from the caterpillar to the butterfly manifesting stage.

QUIRKS: Pluto is like the quiet, intense and goth cousin.

SPECIALTIES: Secrets. Death. Rebirth. Power. Control.

FAVORITE SIGNS: Scorpio

ADVICE: "Even when people tell you that you can't or that you're nothing... use this opportunity to reach deep within and prove them wrong."

Pluto is a small and mighty planet. He is wonderful helping in manifesting. He'll hold your hand in his and escort you to the depths of your soul. He'll shine light into the areas needing a swift demise. Once accomplished, Pluto gives you the fiery energy and tenacious confidence to rise like the phoenix. Working with Pluto, you will soar higher than ever before.

Work with Pluto when you want:

Secret talents revealed. Sometimes you take your gifts for granted. Sometimes you assume your talents are no good. Pluto helps you see that just is not so. Your hidden gifts are begging to come to light. Pluto will help this transformation.

- Set your inner most dreams free
- Release limiting beliefs, habits and hurts and rise like the Phoenix
- Intense and significant change with shadow work

When Pluto is Retrograde

Sometimes you're in a funk. It happens. Pluto Retrograde transforms you. No more wallowing or stuck in the pits. Pluto pulls you out of any pits blocking your manifesting! This covers every area: spiritually, physically, and emotionally.

Navigate Pluto Retrograde

- Explore shadow work (the darker areas of our personality/soul) with the intention of releasing and transforming
- Use this time for honest evaluation in every area of your life to see what you can, or should, release
- Examine areas of control. Are you allowing the magic to flow or exerting control and wanting to manifest your way instead?

Pluto Retrograde for Manifesting

And the truth shall set you free. Pluto retrograde provides the spotlight on the areas causing any manifesting limitations. Whether from a past life or current programing, this is the time to shine the light on the inner constraints. Obliterate the emotional chains of fear, insecurities and doubt. Be open to the confidence and spiritual guidance and accept your inner power. Pluto retrograde will eradicate the obstacles so you can tune into being the manifesting superstar you were created to be.

This retrograde may be just the one to help you manifest what you want!

Scorpio you'll be impacted more than other signs. Pluto Retrograde will reveal your inner secrets -- even the ones you've been keeping from yourself. Apply this energy to shed what's not working and embrace and reclaim your passion and power!

CHIRON

Chiron

Chiron, friendly, loving and compassionate ancient family.
He loves you and frees you to manifest your dreams deepest desires.

QUIRKS: Chiron is like the sensitive, kind, maverick in the family tree.

SPECIALTIES: Healing. Teacher. Abandonment. Compassion.

FAVORITE SIGNS: He doesn't play favorites to ensure no one is left out.

ADVICE: "Heal yourself. Step into your unique greatness and
then you'll be victorious in manifesting your dreams."

Chiron is called a minor planet, comet, and an asteroid. His Greek story
tells of abandonment, betrayal and rejection. A centaur (half-man, half-
horse), Chiron constantly lived a unique path thanks to the upbringing
of his adopted dad, Apollo. Unlike other centaurs who were very much
bullies on the scene, Chiron was a healer, teacher, prophet, and supporter
of the arts. He did not fit in. He teaches that you don't need to either.
Celebrate your uniqueness. Celebrate your calling and your spiritual gifts.

Work with Chiron when you want:

Healing in any area of your life. Chiron knows the challenges of life. He
knows rejection. He knows the path to healing and overcoming adversity,

whether intentional or accidental. Chiron helps make lemonade out of life's lemons.

- Create healing and empowering affirmations
- Explore alternative healing
- Write inspirational and powerful poetry, memoirs and messages

When Chiron is Retrograde

Everyone has deep wounds. Chiron Retrograding is a time to identify and free yourself from any guilt. He helps you see the benefits of this hardship, so you truly walk away feeling stronger and worthy of success.

Navigate Chiron Retrograde

- Celebrate your uniqueness
- Release the hurt, pain, and deep-down rejection once and for all
- Indulge in self-care and schedule daily spoiling

Chiron Retrograde for Manifesting

No faking. No more lying to yourself. Why aren't you manifesting? What is at the core? Lean into this and identify each nook and cranny. Don't rush. Let this be revealed so you can address, release and overcome. Knowing that golden nugget that's been hampering your joy, your success, your dreams will topple over the rest of the blockages. Then write out, pen to paper, why you are worthy of manifesting this dream. Chiron will take this message to the heavens and shout it to the universe!

This retrograde may be just the one to help you manifest what you want!

All signs are impacted. Chiron Retrograde is here to help. Use the gift of this magical, powerful healing time.

Manifesting
WITH THE
Astrological Signs

★

Think of each zodiac sign as bringing its own unique flavor to the cosmic party! Whether it's your sun sign serving up the main dish, your moon sign mixing the mood-enhancing cocktails, or your rising sign DJing the beats, there's a little something for everyone.

In this section, you'll discover how to harness these zesty zodiac vibes to spice up your manifesting mojo! And remember, even if the party's happening elsewhere in the cosmos, those zodiac energies still drop by to sprinkle some stardust on your dreams!".

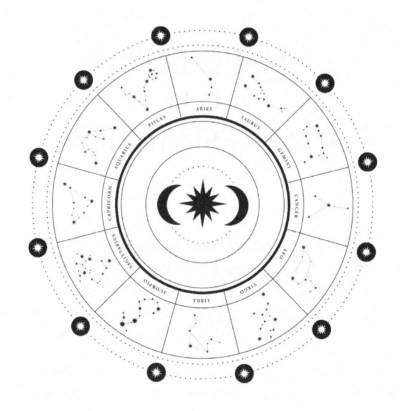

Meanings & Manifesting

Ready for a stellar boost in your manifesting game? Astrology signs are like the universe's secret cheat codes, gifting you cosmic treats and energizing vibes. Think of them as the zodiac's own "power-ups" — be it from your sun sign, the moon's mood swings, or where the stars hang out monthly.

By tuning into these astro-vibes, you're not just going with the flow; you're deliberately tuning into each cosmic currents!

This chapter spills the celestial tea on each sign, their zodiacal zing, and how to channel that into your manifesting goals:

Star Dates: Think of these as zodiac birthdays! Get to know when each sign has its time in the spotlight.

Planet Pals: Did you know each zodiac sign has a buddy planet? Check out who's friends with whom and dive even deeper in the *Planets* section.

Sign Vibes: Dive into the unique personality traits of each sign and how it can light up your life. It's like decoding the character traits of your favorite book's heroes!

Cosmic Choreography: Every sign dances to a unique tempo. It's a celestial dance of initiation, steadfastness, and adaptation. Ready to learn your zodiac's dance steps and groove in harmony with the universe?

Not sure about your star sign?

No worries! Just hop online and search for "natal birth chart." Pop in your birth details (date, time, and place), and voila! Many cool sites will serve up your zodiac sign on a starry platter. And a cheeky tip: if your birthday falls when one sign is passing the baton to another (that's called the "cusp"), it's super important to check – you might get some delightful zodiac surprises!

Bonus Tip: *When the sun dances into your zodiac sign, you're not just on the guest list, you're the VIP! Think of it as the cosmic red carpet rolling out just for you. With the universe's DJ playing your tune, every vibe, and energy syncs to amplify your personal power. Manifesting dreams? It's like you've got a direct line to the universe's backstage crew, ready to turn your wishes into reality. So, when the sun is in your sign, remember to strut your stuff, soak up the vibes, and revel in the universal applause!*

Ready to crank up the volume on the universe's cosmic chords? Let's riff into the zodiac modalities! Think of these as the universe's own rock genres.

1. **Cardinal Signs** *(Aries, Cancer, Libra, Capricorn)* — These are the zodiac's lead singers, always ready to drop the first note and set the stage on fire. They're the ones opening the show, bringing the house down from the get-go! Their cosmic chorus goes, "Strike the chord of change, blaze the trail, and let your inner rockstar steal the spotlight!"

2. **Fixed Signs** *(Taurus, Leo, Scorpio, Aquarius)* — The zodiac's trusty drummers, holding the beat steady and strong. They're the bass line that underpins the whole track, the reliable rhythm you

groove to. Their musical mantra? "Stay in the groove, keep the rhythm, and let your solid beats be the heart of the tune!"

3. **Mutable Signs** (*Gemini, Virgo, Sagittarius, Pisces*) — Ever seen a guitarist do a crazy solo, fingers flying all over the fretboard? That's them! They're the freestyle soloists, jamming and improvising, always ready to switch it up. Their lyrical wisdom? "Ride the rhythm of change, sync with life's beats, and let your versatility steal the show!"

So, strap in and hold tight, because this chapter's about to give you a front-row seat to the celestial concert of the zodiac, turning up the volume on your manifesting mojo!

Aries

Begins on the Equinox, therefore can begin anywhere
from the 19th of March to the 21st of March

TYPICAL SEASON IS: 21 March – 19 April

Download the current dates at www.essentialmanifestingguidebook.com

SPECIALTIES: Energetic. Confident. Natural Leader. Entrepreneur.

FAVORITE PLANET: Mars

MOTTO: I am going to manifest it!

The first sign of the zodiac, Aries comes right out with manifesting power. Mindset and energy are aligned with making their dreams happen. Aries is a wonderful energy for manifesting anything and everything. They have the stamina, focus, and optimistic attitude to accomplish what they want.

ARIES MANIFESTING STRENGTHS

- Creating new business, career, opportunities
- Taking action on unfinished projects, and shelved manifesting dreams
- Overcoming a financial challenge
- Pursuing any solo endeavor or dream
- Making decisions

ARIES IS A **CARDINAL** SIGN

She brings eagerness and drive. Their energy? Unstoppable and undeniably magnetic! They're all about kick-starting and leading the way. How can you apply in your manifesting goals?

TO MANIFEST WITH THIS SIGN

- Know what you want.
- Write 5 ways you can take action to achieve this.
- Take action every day. Aries is all about action taking and accomplishment.
- Stay aligned with Aries

"Embracing Aries' dynamic drive, I manifest with a spirited high-five! With the ram's fearless zest, I harness boldness for manifesting my best!"

Top 3 Crystals for
Aries

1) *Red Jasper:* Need a boost in stamina for your next adventure? This stone has got your back! Plus, it's like a cosmic coffee shot for focus and determination.

2) *Carnelian:* For Aries energy, always ready to lead the charge, carnelian is your ultimate hype-crystal. It's the BFF that whispers, "Go for it!

3) *Diamond:* Shine bright! This isn't just a bling thing – diamond's energy will make you feel unstoppable and looking fab while you're at it.

Taurus

Can begin anywhere from the 19th of April to the 21st of April

TYPICAL SEASON IS: 20 April – 20 May

Download the current dates at www.essentialmanifestingguidebook.com

SPECIALTIES: Loyal. Determined. Romantic.

FAVORITE PLANET: Venus

MOTTO: I am going to have it!

The determination of Taurus provides the tenacity and fortitude to manifest. This is perfect manifesting energy for attracting the finer things in life. Creative, strong and determined, Taurus will help you have the perfect plan and the energy to stay the course.

TAURUS MANIFESTING STRENGTHS

- Obtaining the finer things
- Increased creativity
- Energy and stubbornness to keep going
- Love and beauty

TAURUS IS A **FIXED** SIGN

She brings grace and determination. She anchors and carries out what was begun by the Cardinal signs. She is the embodiment of dedication and tenacity. How can you apply in your manifesting goals?

TO MANIFEST WITH THIS SIGN

Create a nice meal with all the scrumptiousness. This includes candles, pleasant music, nice plates, candles, linen napkins. Include a beautiful crystal or sentimental glass. This should feel extremely luxurious.

Thoroughly enjoy this exquisite connection.

As you're feeling appreciative of the moment, answer this: What would you want if money was no object? What would you truly want?

If it's been a while or you're so tuned out of your heart's desires, Taurus will help you remember the beautiful things, the loving relationship, and the joy of your exquisite soul.

When you're tuning into the gifts of the Taurus energy, you're tuning into the talents of Leonardo da Vinci, Kelly Clarkson, and Dwayne Johnson who are all encouraging you to dream bigger!

"Channeling Taurus' steadfast might, I manifest with grounded delight! With the bull's patient grace, I create dreams at a winning pace!"

Top 3 Crystals for Taurus

1) *Emerald:* The birthstone for May, this gem isn't just for royals. It resonates with Taurus energy, promoting loyalty, unity, and a big dash of elegance.

2) *Pyrite:* Another one for luxury-loving energy of Taurus! Known as "Fool's Gold," this stone attracts wealth and abundance – because who says you can't enjoy the finer things?

3) *Tiger's Eye:* Add a bit of fierceness, shall we? This stone boosts your confidence and helps keep those determined Taurean eyes on the prize.

Gemini

Can begin anywhere from the 20th of May to the 21st of May

TYPICAL SEASON IS: 21 May – 20 June

Download the current dates at www.essentialmanifestingguidebook.com

SPECIALTIES: Social. Curious. Spontaneous. Chatty.

FAVORITE PLANET: Mercury

MOTTO: I am going to talk it into manifesting!

Dazzling, chatty, zipping around Gemini will help you manifest without all the limitations of doing it "the right way." Playful Gemini helps your vibration remain high. The twins will help you have twice the manifesting energy if you'll let them!

GEMINI MANIFESTING STRENGTHS

- Being flexible and open-minded
- Reaching out, exploring and networking new opportunities
- Ability to manifest several things at once
- Communicating the best manifesting thoughts and affirmations

GEMINI IS A **MUTABLE** SIGN

She brings flexibility and versatility. She prepares for the transition to the next season, next steps and next phases. How can you apply in your manifesting goals?

TO MANIFEST WITH THIS SIGN

Communicate your manifesting desires. Know what you want. Script your thoughts and affirmations around that. Remember, Gemini is quick-minded. She's not going to linger on any affirmation. Neither will you! Write it down. Next!

"Embracing Gemini's twin-power flair, I manifest with double the air! With the twins' vibrant chat, I attract my desires, just like that!"

Top 3 Crystals for Gemini

1) *Agate:* Just like the dual nature of Gemini, agate comes in many colors and layers. It's all about balance, harmonizing yin and yang, and... it's basically like a mood ring for your soul!

2) *Citrine:* Need a mental lift-off? Citrine is your go-to brain booster, supercharging that already radiant intellect and vibrant energy.

3) *Tiger's Eye:* Ooh, shiny! This stone offers clarity and insight, which, let's face it, is always welcome when you're juggling a million ideas at once.

Cancer

Can begin anywhere from the 20th of June to the 22nd of June

TYPICAL SEASON IS: 21 June – 22 July

Download the current dates at www.essentialmanifestingguidebook.com

SPECIALTIES: Emotional. Homebody. Super Psychic.

FAVORITE PLANET: Moon

MOTTO: I am going to nurture it into manifesting!

This water sign is ruled by the Moon! It's no wonder that this sign is a natural nurturer! Represented by the crab, Cancer's energy provides a wonderful opportunity to evaluate your boundaries!

CANCER MANIFESTING STRENGTHS

- Superhero intuition abilities...they just know that they know
- Nurturing through the calm and rough waters
- Home and family
- Successful small businesses and start-ups
- Knowing when you need to withdraw and nurture you

CANCER IS A **CARDINAL** SIGN

She brings eagerness and drive. Their energy? Unstoppable and undeniably magnetic! They're all about kick-starting and leading the way. How can you apply in your manifesting goals?

TO MANIFEST WITH THIS SIGN

Connect with Cancer energy in the shower, in the bath, or watching a water fountain. Look at the flow. This will be a time when your ideas are especially bountiful in the shower. Cancer has the natural abilities to go with the flow, step out, and hide within when needed and use their pincers to grasp and hold on.

Slipping a moonstone into your pocket creates a subtle connection to this sensitive sign. Keep carrying it until you've reached your goal. Even if the sun moves into other signs, Cancer will continue to support you until you've manifested this desire.

"Tapping into Cancer's moonlit tide, I manifest with a nurturing stride! With the crab's heartfelt care, I cocoon my dreams and let them flare!"

Top 3 Crystals for
Cancer

1) *Moonstone:* A no-brainer for Moon children!
Moonstone tunes into your deep intuition,
amplifies your emotional intelligence, and has all
those lunar vibes you adore.

2) *Rhodonite:* Think of it as your emotional
lifebuoy. When emotions ebb and flow, Rhodonite
keeps you afloat, promoting balance and
grounding.

3) *Calcite:* Like a spa day for your soul. Relax,
rejuvenate, and refresh with this calming stone.

Leo

Can begin anywhere from the 22nd of July to the 23rd of July

TYPICAL SEASON IS: 23 July – 22 August

Download the current dates at www.essentialmanifestingguidebook.com

SPECIALTIES: Bold. Courageous. Warmhearted.

FAVORITE PLANET: Sun

MOTTO: I am deserving of it being manifested!

Confident and Optimistic, Leo has the manifesting success spotlight. Popular, Leo is able to stand out in a crowd because of its gorgeous, presence and loyalty. Leos are exceedingly generous. Leo shares the manifesting spotlight.

LEO MANIFESTING STRENGTHS

- Courage to pursue dreams, even outlandish ones
- Playful and creative
- Stepping into your light
- Ambitious
- Able to excel and stand out in the crowd

LEO IS A **FIXED** SIGN

She brings grace and determination. She anchors and carries out what was begun by the Cardinal signs. She is the embodiment of dedication and tenacity. How can you apply in your manifesting goals?

TO MANIFEST WITH THIS SIGN

Imagine taking center stage. Lights are all on you. There is no fear... even if you have a history of stage fright. Leo is by you. Interviewing you. Sharing your success story with the world. In fact, Leo knows every juicy detail of your perseverance, your manifesting journey, and is singing your praises. Compliments are flowing.

"Channeling Leo's radiant sun, I manifest and have tons of fun! With the lion's regal roar, my dreams take center stage and soar!"

Top 3 Crystals for
Leo

1) Tiger's Eye: Channel your inner big cat with this gem! 🐅 It's all about courage, confidence, and strutting your stuff with style.

2) Citrine: Like a shot of espresso for your spirit, Citrine boosts your natural charisma and amps up that sunny disposition. It's basically sunshine in crystal form.

3) Peridot: A confidence boost in crystal form, lighting up your inner royalty. Perfect for Leo energy looking for that extra sprinkle of self-worth and prosperity. Shine on!

Virgo

Can begin anywhere from the 22nd of August to the 23rd of August

TYPICAL SEASON IS: **23 August – 22 September**

Download the current dates at www.essentialmanifestingguidebook.com

SPECIALTIES: Organized. Practical. Perfectionist. Helpful.

FAVORITE PLANET: Mercury

MOTTO: I've got a plan to manifest it!

Practical Virgo not only has a plan, she has a perfect, efficient plan. She can sort through a jumbled mess and connect the dots. Chaos doesn't belong in Virgo's world, so manifesting plans will be focused and simple to do. She'll also remind you of the importance of taking care of yourself so you can be healthy and enjoy your dreams manifested.

VIRGO MANIFESTING STRENGTHS

- Increased health and healing touch
- Exploring new skills
- Success whenever she puts her mind to it
- Implementing the right way

VIRGO IS A **MUTABLE** SIGN

She brings flexibility and versatility. She prepares for the transition to the next season, next steps and next phases. How can you apply in your manifesting goals?

TO MANIFEST WITH THIS SIGN

Decide what you want to manifest and recruit Virgo's assistance. She'll create a plan and strategy to expertly achieve it. Preferring a system, Virgo ties in the manifesting steps perfectly.

1. Focused intentional thoughts.
2. Focused intentional actions.
3. Focused intentional manifesting.

Virgo will help you stay organized with your eyes on the prize.

"Embracing Virgo's meticulous vibe, I manifest with precision and thrive! With the maiden's detailed sight, my dreams align just right!"

Top 3 Crystals for
Virgo

1) *Moss Agate:* Just like its name suggests, this stone is all about growth, grounding, and embracing Mother Nature. It's like a green thumb in crystal form.

2) *Sapphire:* Associated with wisdom and insight, Sapphire is Virgo's best friend when seeking clarity and focus. It's like having a guiding star on those late work nights or during contemplative moments.

3) *Fluorite:* It's your organizational buddy! Fluorite can help Virgos channel their natural ability to structure and declutter.

Libra

Can begin anywhere from the 22nd of September to the 23rd of September

TYPICAL SEASON IS: 23 September – 22 October

Download the current dates at www.essentialmanifestingguidebook.com

SPECIALTIES: Balanced. Diplomatic. Kind.

FAVORITE PLANET: Venus

MOTTO: There's plenty for all of us to manifest!

Libra wants a win for all. She's fair-minded, compromising and tactful. Charming Librans are able to gently turn any situation around because at the center of it all is... love. Like the famous Libran, Ghandi, this sign will peacefully reconnect everything with love. Love is that high vibration which makes for being a manifesting magnet.

LIBRA MANIFESTING STRENGTHS

- Creating a peaceful home, office, environment
- Calmness and adaptability
- Understanding a situation to help forgive and heal
- Believing it is possible
- Harmony

LIBRA IS A **CARDINAL** SIGN

She brings eagerness and drive. Their energy? Unstoppable and undeniably magnetic! They're all about kick-starting and leading the way. How can you apply in your manifesting goals?

TO MANIFEST WITH THIS SIGN

Use the arts to connect with Libra. Grab a paint brush and canvas. Dance to classical music. Visit an art museum. Enjoy the joie de vivre as you connect with this Goddess Venus-ruled sign.

Manifest the love, beauty, and harmony into your life.

"Channeling Libra's harmonious scale, I manifest with a balanced trail! With the sign of the scales leading my quest, my dreams find balance and manifest at their best!"

Top 3 Crystals for
Libra

1) Lepidolite: Need zen? This pretty lilac crystal is like yoga for the soul. Libra-approved tranquility in gem form!

2) Opal: This iridescent gem promotes creativity and expression. Perfect for those who love a dash of artistic flair!

3) Jade: Think of Jade as your harmonious BFF whispering, "You got this, and you look fabulous doing it!"

Scorpio

Can begin anywhere from the 22nd of October to the 23rd of October

TYPICAL SEASON IS: 23 October – 21 November

Download the current dates at www.essentialmanifestingguidebook.com

SPECIALTIES: Passionate, Intuitive. Secretive.

FAVORITE PLANETS: Mars and Pluto

MOTTO: I demand it and it is manifested!

This water sign is mysterious, intimidating and magical. Ruled by Mars until Pluto stepped out of her shadow, Scorpio has a shroud of secrecy. And, Scorpio just *knows* things. Their intuitive inside tract is manifesting intensity. They set themselves up to succeed and will push it to the unknown to achieve it.

SCORPIO MANIFESTING STRENGTHS

- Intelligent and imaginative
- Know how to get what you want
- Transformation
- Self-control
- Stretching for the deep desires of our soul

SCORPIO IS A **FIXED** SIGN

She brings grace and determination. She anchors and carries out what was begun by the Cardinal signs. She is the embodiment of dedication and tenacity. How can you apply in your manifesting goals?

TO MANIFEST WITH THIS SIGN

Explore working with a tarot deck or pendulum. Even if you've never picked either up, going into this deep territory brings psychic Scorpio along. Give yourself a reading and see the truth this honest sign delivers.

"Drawing from Scorpio's deep mystique, I manifest goals that peak! With the scorpion's transformative sting, I power through and make my dreams sing!"

Top 3 Crystals for Scorpio

1) Topaz: Glowing with energy and brilliance, just like Scorpio energy! Topaz brings joy, generosity, and abundance. It's like having a sunbeam in your pocket, reminding you to shine your light even in the deepest waters.

2) Rhodochrosite: This pink beauty is like a love letter to your heart. It's the perfect match for plunging deep into emotions. When the waters get a tad stormy, this gem's here to remind you that love, both given and received, can heal all.

3) Obsidian: This crystal is like your personal security guard. It protects and wards off negativity. Plus, it's as intense and deep as your favorite dark chocolate.

Sagittarius

Can begin anywhere from the 21st of November to the 22nd of November

TYPICAL SEASON IS: 22 November – 21 December

Download the current dates at www.essentialmanifestingguidebook.com

SPECIALTIES: Adventurous. Inquisitive. Honest.

FAVORITE PLANET: Jupiter

MOTTO: Why do a subtle manifesting when you can go all the way?

This centaur brings the wild acceptance and thrill of your manifesting journey. Her optimism, openness, and excitement toward the possibilities allow to truly manifest "this or something better." She is a perpetual student and teacher so she's constantly learning new approaches to manifesting a wonderful life.

SAGITTARIUS MANIFESTING STRENGTHS

- Taking manifesting dreams to the next level
- Freedom and independence
- Humor
- Exploring new territory

SAGITTARIUS IS A **MUTABLE** SIGN

She brings flexibility and versatility. She prepares for the transition to the next season, next steps in manifesting, next phases. How can you apply in your manifesting goals?

TO MANIFEST WITH THIS SIGN

Explore new territory! This wanderlust sign brings the fun in discovering and learning. Travel outside and uncover new perspectives. Lie on the ground and look from a cat's point of view. Go horseback riding and look from the (almost) centaur's view. Or watch a documentary on the Andes. Explore the new with the curiosity and excitement of Sagittarius.

"Channeling Sagittarius' adventurous spree, I manifest with wild and boundless glee! With the archer's aim so true, I shoot for the stars and my dreams come into view!"

Top 3 Crystals for
Sagittarius

1) *Blue Topaz:* A gem that's all heart, signifying love and affection. It's your go-to for balancing emotions and thoughts, ensuring your fiery spirit enjoys harmonious vibes. Perfect for seeking both passion and peace.

2) *Turquoise:* Wanderlust on your mind? Turquoise, known as the traveler's stone, is your passport to protection and good fortune on your adventures!

3) *Amethyst:* A touch of spirituality for those who love to explore the mysteries of the universe. Plus, it's so pretty—double win!

Capricorn

Can begin anywhere from the 21st of December to the 22nd of December

TYPICAL SEASON IS: 22 December – 19 January

Download the current dates at www.essentialmanifestingguidebook.com

SPECIALTIES: Responsible. Hard working, Planner

FAVORITE PLANET: Saturn

MOTTO: Ain't no mountain high enough...
to keep me from manifesting what I want.

"If it ain't broke don't fix it," could be mumbled under Capricorn's breath. She's not going to waste time when there's a mountain to climb or a dream to achieve. There's a traditional way that works. Capricorn brings the "A" game, especially when needing laser focus to manifest one thing. You'll enjoy sharing the manifesting journey with this self-aware, natural leader.

CAPRICORN MANIFESTING STRENGTHS

- Extremely driven and extremely successful
- Manifesting for the long haul
- Able to remain focused until the dream is achieved
- Practical skills and clear goals for swift manifesting
- Detail-oriented and able to make quick adjustments

CAPRICORN IS A **CARDINAL** SIGN

She brings eagerness and drive. Their energy? Unstoppable and undeniably magnetic! They're all about kick-starting and leading the way. How can you apply in your manifesting goals?

TO MANIFEST WITH THIS SIGN

Consider revisiting some of the original, everyday skills like sewing, carpentry, cooking, or gardening, skills that used to be the norm. These activities unlock memories and manifesting techniques. Capricorn doesn't mind the hard work and they expect the outcome they desire. Embrace your manifesting steps to make the most of this self-sufficient manifesting energy.

Embracing Capricorn's steadfast climb, I manifest one step at a time! With the mountain goat's sturdy stance, my dreams find grounding and a chance to dance!"

Top 3 Crystals for
Capricorn

1) *Green Tourmaline:* Abundance alert! This gem is all about attracting prosperity and success. Plus, it's great for heart healing and balance. Capricorn knows hard work deserves rich rewards, Green Tourmaline is your prosperity partner in sparkle!

2) *Jet:* Think of Jet as your protective shield, absorbing negativity and easing emotional stress. Jet offers a gentle grounding, ensuring that even amidst life's storms, you stand firm and centered. It's like having a wise old tree as your personal guardian, keeping you rooted while you reach for the stars

3) *Malachite:* Like a personal life coach in crystal form, Malachite encourages growth, clears out the old, and paves the way for new adventures. Bold leaps, hear you come!

Aquarius

Can begin anywhere from the 19th of January to the 20th of January

TYPICAL SEASON IS: 20 January – 18 February

Download the current dates at www.essentialmanifestingguidebook.com

SPECIALTIES: Intelligent. Quirky. Humanitarian.

FAVORITE PLANET: Uranus

MOTTO: Let's all manifest!

They love the crowd. Aquarius enjoys being a musketeer, all for one and one for all and please still give me my space. This dreamer is able to see the good that belongs to tomorrow. This is especially helpful when you're going through a difficulty, because Aquarius is able to provide hope.

AQUARIUS MANIFESTING STRENGTHS

- Incorporating technology
- Ideas that will benefit many
- Able to keep relaxed and confident about the outcome
- Scientific approach
- Detail-oriented and able to make quick adjustments

AQUARIUS IS A **FIXED** SIGN

She brings grace and determination. She anchors and carries out what was begun by the Cardinal signs. She is the embodiment of dedication and tenacity. How can you apply in your manifesting goals?

TO MANIFEST WITH THIS SIGN

This is a great time to manifest for the future. Starting a family, funds for retirement, or opening a rescue shelter, Aquarius will lend a helping hand. This is the time to implement the Cosmic Happenings for manifesting. This is right in Aquarius's wheelhouse. Pay attention to any online courses or connections Aquarius sends to you and stay open to the unexpected.

"Channeling Aquarius' innovative flow, I manifest with a futuristic glow! With the water bearer's visionary sight, my dreams take flight in neon light!"

Top 3 Crystals for
Aquarius

1) *Tektite:* As one-of-a-kind as you are! This tektite is a about rapid transformation and celestial connection.

2) *Amethyst:* A stone of intuition and spiritual insight. Perfect for the Aquarius who's always gazing ahead!

3) *Labradorite:* Unleash your magical potential and trust the universe's flow. It's like having a wand, but in gem form.

Pisces

Can begin anywhere from the 18th of February to the 19th of February

TYPICAL SEASON IS: 19 February – 20 March

Download the current dates at www.essentialmanifestingguidebook.com

SPECIALTIES: Intuitive. Artistic. Magical.

FAVORITE PLANET: Neptune and Jupiter

MOTTO: I go with the flow and I end up with
my dreams manifested! Let me help you!

The last sign of the zodiac, Pisces swims up and helps everyone. Wanting to provide assistance whether wanting to help you manifest health, money, or love, Pisces is there. It understands the ancient alchemy. It'll share alternative, creative, manifesting ideas. Compassionate and sensitive, Pisces is a natural empath. She believes in you and in your dreams. She'll do all she can to help... after her nap.

PISCES MANIFESTING STRENGTHS

- Exploring past lives to eliminate blockages
- Exploring past lives to remember success
- Able to find the best vibrational current

- Highly intuitive, they'll guide you to the perfect crystal or essential oil
- Able to take breaks and recharge (this really is a huge, beneficial strength)

PISCES IS A **MUTABLE** SIGN

She brings flexibility and versatility. She prepares for the transition to the next season, next steps and next phases. How can you apply in your manifesting goals?

TO MANIFEST WITH THIS SIGN

Record your own meditations. You can write your affirmations and record them or create your own full meditation. Then, rest. Snuggle. Doze. Pay attention to any intuitive dreams, for Pisces will continue to inspire you.

"Drawing from Pisces' dreamy seas, I manifest with fluid ease! With the fish guiding my intuitive dance, my dreams swirl into life with a mystical trance!"

**Top 3 Crystals for
Pisces**

1) Amethyst: The ultimate dream stone. Enhance your intuition and keep those creative juices flowing. Perfect for a Piscean vision quest!

2) Aquamarine: Soothing sea vibes, anyone? Aquamarine offers clarity and emotional healing—like a spa day for your soul.

3) Sodalite: Unlock your innermost dreams and channel that vast Piscean imagination. It's like your personal muse in crystal form!

Manifesting
with the
Moon

★

Step into the moonlit realm and let's dive deep into the moon's enchanting mysteries. In this section, we're uncovering all the sparkly secrets of her magic. The moon, our cosmic BFF, is always brimming with insights, discoveries, and a sprinkle of moon-dust guidance. Whether she's waxing, waning, or just shining bright, her vibes are ever-ready to give your manifesting journey a glow-up! While the universe always has its ears perked up for your dreams, harmonizing with the moon's rhythm sprinkles a little extra starlight on your wishes. With the moon's magic in hand, not only does the impossible become possible, but it also becomes a moonlit dance of dreams and delight!"

THE MOON

Meanings &
Manifesting Energies

A h, the moon, our celestial goddess, radiant and regal in her silver splendor! As she dances across the night sky, she weaves a tapestry of dreams, binding us with threads of ancient wisdom and timeless wonder. From her sway over the tides to the rhythm of our very souls, she's the universe's nurturing mother, singing lullabies of love and lore.

Ever flicked through history's pages? You'd spot our ancestors dancing to the moon's tune. From ancient lunar calendars etched into stone to moonlit tales painted on sacred cave walls, they've left us breadcrumbs of their lunar love affair. And the coolest part? You don't need to don a time-traveling hat to groove to these age-old rhythms. The cosmic dance floor is ever open, and the moon's magic is an invite that never expires!

Engaging with the moon is like finding your rhythm in the universe's grand symphony, setting you on a golden track of manifesting stardom.

A Lunar Look-Back

Our celestial queen has seen it all. Though she's a timeless beauty, she's been swaying in the cosmic winds for a cool 4.53 billion years. Nestled a mere 238,000 miles away, she serenades us with her ethereal glow night after night.

The realm of Cancer is her astro-turf, but her lunar lullabies sing to every sign under the stars. Delve into her domain, and you'll discover a world of emotion, intuition, and some celestial TLC. She embodies the divine feminine, diving deep into the seas of the soul, guiding us through introspection and intimacy.

Think of her as the universe's nurturing nanny, holding your hand, whispering sweet nothings, and encouraging you to spread those spiritual wings. Whatever heart's desire you're yearning to bring into reality, the Moon is your cosmic co-conspirator, always ready to lend her manifesting magic.

And here's a fun fact to sprinkle into your stargazing sessions: Our Ice Age ancestors were so moon-smitten, they were crafting lunar calendars some 34,000 years ago! So next time you gaze up, remember you're joining a tradition as old as time.

Working with the moon and her cycles truly allows you to place yourself in the nurturing flow of manifesting success.

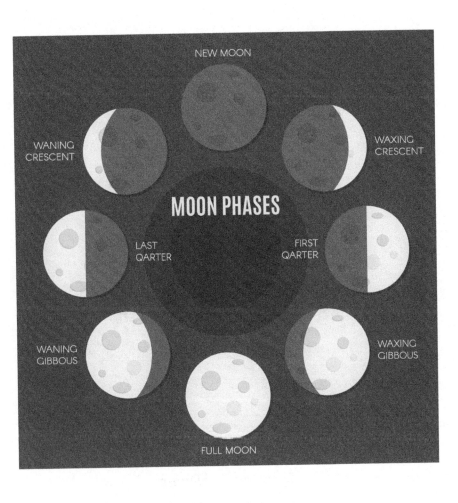

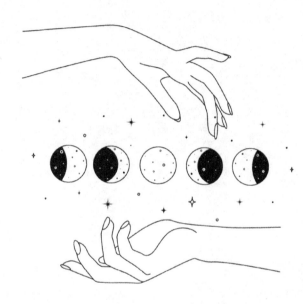

*Every moon phase is a page
in the story of your
manifesting stage.*

Working with the Cycles of the Moon

New Moon is when the moon is not visible in the sky. This marks a fresh start. It is a time for planting new seeds of desires, setting new intentions, and conceiving new dreams that you want to manifest.

First Quarter is when the moon looks half full. This is the time for going all in emotionally and physically. This is the time of laser focus and taking action toward manifesting.

Full Moon is when the moon is totally full! You've come a long way, baby! You've put in the work. Celebrate all that has happened. Fill your soul with gratitude. Allow the full moon to illuminate any areas that can be tweaked. This is a great time to read your cards, ask angels for divine insight, and meditate on your dream already manifested.

Last Quarter is when the moon is half full. Assess your progress. What changes are necessary. How can you modify under the next New Moon cycle. Begin to release what is no longer supporting your manifesting desires.

Waxing is the moon cycle from the New Moon to the Full Moon. Energy increases during this time. This is the time for building, increasing, and growth.

Waning is the moon cycle from Full Moon to New Moon. Energy is diminishing. This is a time of releasing what isn't working and allowing it to be subtly released and pulled away.

Lunar Eclipse is when the Earth's shadow is blocking the sun's light. The light is stopped. Lunar Eclipse is a time to go within, unlike a solar eclipse which impacts your physical body and taking action. This Lunar Eclipse is the time to get emotionally naked. The truth is there to be seen. What isn't serving you anymore? What emotional cycle is blocking your manifesting? Address and release for a swift and total emotional prosperous shift. *Eclipses deliver powerful and accelerated change.*

Supermoon is when the moon is at its closest point to the Earth. During this time, the moon is 30% brighter and 14% larger than a Micromoon and is 16% brighter than a usual moon. This occurs as a *Super New Moon* and a *Super Full Moon*. During these occasions the moon's manifesting aspects and energies are intensified.

Micromoon is when the moon is farthest from the Earth. During this time, the moon will look smaller and less bright. During these occasions, the moon's manifesting energies lend themselves to small teaks to your manifesting. Actions taken during this time will create steady and sustainable results.

A *Supermoon* and *Micromoon* both impact the ocean's tides. A *Supermoon* increases the water 5 cm or 2" and a *Micromoon* decreases the tides the same amount.

Enhancing Your
Moon Connection

H ave you ever stopped to think about how our ancestors were totally moonstruck? I mean, back in the day, they'd plan their entire lives around its glow — from epic rituals to deciding when to plant crops. That's some major moon love!

Now, here's the cool bit: just like how the moon plays puppeteer with the ocean tides, it has this sneaky way of syncing up with our inner vibes. Ladies, in particular, might feel this link pretty deeply. Ever had one of those days where you just felt... lunar? It's all connected!

Here's how the moon can jazz up our manifesting mojo: Every new moon is like a cosmic reset button, perfect for setting sparkly intentions. As it grows, it's all about getting things rolling. By the time we hit the full moon, it's our big reveal moment! Then, as the moon starts to chill and shrink, it's our cue to kick back, reflect, and prep for the next cycle.

So, next time you're gazing up at that big, glowing disc in the sky, remember: it's not just about the moon up there. It's a dance between its energy, our heartbeats, and all the moonlit memories of folks who came before us.

And here's the real kicker: by tuning into the moon's rhythms and aligning our intentions with its phases, we supercharge our manifesting game. It's like tapping into an ancient, cosmic Wi-Fi — the connection is stronger, clearer, and just... magical. By syncing up with the moon, we're not just hoping for our dreams to manifest, we're working in tandem with the universe. It's a partnership, a dance, and trust me, the universe has got some killer dance moves. So harness that moon magic, make your dreams a reality, and rock the cosmic stage together!

Here are some simple ways to energetically connect with the moon:

1. Sit outside under the night sky.

Find the perfect, comfortable spot. Sitting on a chair or a blanket, gaze into the sky and find the moon. Notice her current cycle and whether she's in the waxing or waning period. Both bring energy and clarity.

Take a cleansing breath as you ground your energy by connecting with earth below you. Take another cleansing breath as you imagine sending a stream of pink light from your heart all the way to the moon. Imagine her welcoming it and receiving it. Imagine she sends beams of love and connection back to you. Connect with this energy. When you feel like you are bathing in her light, take another cleansing breath. Thank her for her guidance and wisdom. Remember, even if you don't see her light, she is always in the sky.

2. Work with a crystal.

Any crystal will do. Moonstone, Opal, and Labradorite are my favorite for connecting with the powerful goddess energy. Goddess energy provides love, nurturing, strength, and the intuitive power to know how to manifest.

Choose the crystal that you intuitively feel you want to use for your moon connection. Hold it in both of your hands. As you're holding the crystal, close your eyes. Feel any energy in the crystal. When you're ready, ask the moon to imbue her energy into this crystal.

Perhaps you'll feel a warmth or tingles in your hands. Perhaps it will only be a knowing that the connection is there. Slip this crystal into your pocket. Every time you feel, touch, or see your crystal, know that you have this magical connection.

3. Bathe in the moonlight.

Find the area where moon is streaming in through your window or door. Snuggle into the light. As you feel the light shining on you, state affirmations or things you appreciate and love about yourself. Journal eight things (eight is a magical manifesting number) you're grateful for since you have manifested your dreams!

4. Give yourself an oracle reading in the moonlight.

The moon will provide the intuition and answers. By using an oracle deck to get a closer connection, you'll open the door to her manifesting energy and communication.

Take a cleansing breath while holding your deck between your palms. Ask for clarity on what you want to manifest. You can lay down one, three, or as many cards as you'd like. Trust your intuition with the divine message.

I like to do the one or three cards. The one card reading I feel is usually pretty straightforward. When I lay down the three cards, often, the first is my emotional blockage from the past, the second is the present message I need to hear, and the last is the advice to go forward.

Keep track of the message and symbols or images that stood out to you.

5. Make moon water.

Moon water is water imbued with the energy of the moon's cycle and the blessing each cycle brings.

Using a clean glass jar or other glass container, fill it with water. (I use distilled water, but any water is fine.) Put the glass outside in the moon's path and leave overnight. Bring the glass in the next morning. Label your jar so you know which cycle you captured. Store in a dark cabinet.

Use this water for amplifying the moon's manifesting energy.

- Dab it on your crystal, third eye, or throat chakra
- Add it to your bath
- Pour into your diffuser and add essential oils for an extra manifesting boost

Essential oil blends I like:

- New Moon – Orange, Clary Sage, and Frankincense
- First Quarter – Peppermint, Grapefruit, and Lemon
- Full Moon – Ylang Ylang, Sandalwood, and Rose
- Last Quarter – Rosemary, Lemongrass, and Palo Santo

DISCLAIMER: *Always check with your doctor if you have any medical concerns, issues, or allergies. Always check the safety data before using any essential oils. Always use additional caution during pregnancy and with children and pets.*

Harnessing the Moon Cycles for Manifesting

New Moon

This is the beginning of the manifesting cycle. You've done your part to make sure you have good manifesting soil (your mindset and emotions are aligned with receiving). This is the time to set new intentions of what you want to manifest. This always carries the energy of new.

Dates, astrological signs, and times for the new moon are included later in this section under the *Moon Cycles*. Manifesting suggestions for each specific new moon are also included later in the *Moon Cycles* section.

New moon topics for manifesting are focused on the new energies and fresh starts. This is superb for even reviving a stale relationship, seemingly dried-up opportunities, and new confidence or faith in manifesting.

To manifest with the new moon, write your New Moon Intention in a journal or someplace you will have access to throughout the moon cycle. **This is to be handwritten.** You want your connection and energy flowing into the seeds you want to prosper.

Hold your New Moon Intention in your hands and place against your heart. Offer gratitude for this manifested.

Say something like, *"These are my New Moon intentions. I promise to stay open to the divine guidance so this may manifest easier and faster. I know my desires have already come true. It is with much appreciation and gratitude, and with harm to none, that I receive this or something better lovingly manifested. Thank you."*

Put this New Moon Intention where you can easily access it and where the moon will shine through the window offering its growing light. Even if the moon isn't streaming through that window, the moon illuminates the sky and the light will touch your intention sheet.

I like placing mine in my sacred space. However, before I had a sacred space, I used my windowsill or on my nightstand next to my bed.

Super charge your New Moon Intention sheet by adding items that amplify the manifesting energy to your sheet.

- symbols of what you want manifested (like a heart for love, loose change for more wealth, a smiley face for joy)
- crystals
- chimes
- mirror
- glitter
- any items you intuitively feel

Crescent Moon

Within a day or two, the crescent moon begins lending her energy. This is easy to identify. You'll see the sliver of the moon that looks like a sideways Mona Lisa smile. This smile increases and is at its complete crescent phase within 7 days.

This is a time to commit to your intention. Gather wisdom from the cosmic energy being offered like the astrological sign and month's energy, write affirmations or light a candle.

When writing affirmations, remember to state in positive terms and as though it's already materialized.

Let's say you want to manifest money. Your affirmation could be, *"My income is constantly increasing."* Or *"I am prosperous."*

When adding a candle, be deliberate about your choice. Which intuitively feels like the right candle for your new moon intentions? Does size, shape or color matter? Do you want to make your own? Soy vs. Beeswax? Or does that not matter and you know the perfect candle?

Once your candle is chosen, hold the candle between both hands and bless it by saying,

"I bless you and thank you for sharing your manifesting energy."

At this point, you can place with your new moon intention sheet and this phase is concluded.

You can also go another step by lighting your candle.

If you choose to light your candle, set your candle on a safe, flat surface. (Upon your intention sheet if possible)

Light your candle and state, *"This light is special and will shine bright, blessing my dreams each and every night."*

Take a moment and imagine your dreams manifested. Visualize how that looks and feels. Stay visualizing until you intuitively feel that you have connected with this manifestation. You may find a smile suddenly appearing on your face!

Blow out your candle and as the smoke swirls upward say, *"Thank you angels for manifesting this or something better."*

Leave the sheet and candle for the entire moon cycle.

CANDLE COLORS

Here are color meanings according to our ancient ancestors for your reference. Always trust your intuition when choosing.

- Yellow: wisdom, spirituality, sun
- Green: spring, rebirth, wealth
- Blue: improved health, clear skies, opportunities
- Orange: power, movement, endurance
- Red: passion, hope, love
- Brown: happiness, good harvest, healthy foundation
- Purple: faith, belief
- Pink: success
- Black: remembrance

First Quarter Moon

This is when the moon looks half-full. This is 7–10 days from the New Moon. This is the waxing period as the moon increases on its way to becoming full. The first quarter moon for every month is listed later within this section, as well as in the month-at-a-glance section.

This is a time to take action! Analyze what's working and what isn't and make any adjustments. Create additional action steps and release any tension with a good belly laugh. Manifesting is fun, not another job or task to be completed.

This is a perfect time to slip in some confidence-boosting techniques.

MIRROR WORK

Do this first thing in the morning and last thing at night and every time you pass a mirror. Look at yourself and declare that you are worthy. Choose from one of the following or create one of your own.

"I am deserving and worthy of my dreams."
"It is safe me to stand out and shine."
"I am a beautiful, priceless treasure."

CHOOSE YOUR THEME SONG

What type of song is your happy place? Quick tempo? Slow? Instrumental? Sing along?

Set your timer. No overthinking. Choose your theme song.

Once you've decided, give it a go and listen to your theme song.

Still loving it? Great! Now, strike a power pose in front of the mirror as your song plays. Hold this pose for as long as you're able. Let the pose and music blend into this powerful moment. Anytime you hear your theme song, remember to the world you are a super hero and the universe is picking you!

HERE ARE 2 POWER POSES

1. *Super Hero!* Feet grounded, hands on hip, chin up and chest out.

2. *Pick Me!* Feet planted on the ground, raise your arms straight up over your head (like the arm motion for the "Y" in the song "YMCA" by Village People) Turn your palms and face up to the sky. Smile.

Full Moon

The moon is seen completely round and easy to spot in the night sky.

This is the time to review your new moon intentions. See what modifications come to light. The full moon is the goddess energy. She has the higher view and is able to lovingly illuminate any hidden fears, forgotten steps, and areas needing adjustments. Trust this guidance. Take action and get back on track.

Each full moon is in an astrological sign which contributes a unique manifesting energy. Dates, sign and times are included later in this section and with manifesting suggestions in the month-at-a-glance section.

Here are two ways to connect with the full moon.

SELF-CARE HOUR

Just like the full moon is fully round, give yourself a full sixty minutes focused on you. This can be anything from reading your favorite romance novel to enjoying your favorite tv show. Make this deliberate and active.

Here are some other ideas.

- Get a manicure
- Make a smoothie
- Garden
- Snuggle with your pet

CREATE A MANDALA

Mandala literally means "circle" and is from the ancient Sanskrit language. Circles have been drawn forever in nature. When you draw your circle you're connecting with the energy of the universe, including the moon.

Grab your supplies (blank paper and pencils) and get comfortable.

- Visualize the full moon.
- Draw a circle on your paper.
- Visualize your intention manifested.
- Once you feel the joy of this manifested, begin drawing within your circle.

- This can be a scene, splashes of color, symbols, or even more circles. Trust your intuitive creativity. Go with the flow and draw.

No critiquing or judging your work. This is an intimate connection with the moon. Your mandala is coming out exactly as it's supposed to.

Draw until you feel complete. When finished, admire your work. See if there are any hidden images or messages within your art. Is there a color you're naturally drawn to. Even if nothing stands out, compliment yourself for this wonderful union with the moon and your dreams.

Put your mandala someplace safe.

You can also choose a mandala coloring book, coloring page, or grab chalk and color the sidewalk. Whatever method, the healing benefits remain (lowering anxiety and stress, stabilizing blood pressure) and you get closer to the moon!

Last Quarter Moon (also called Third Quarter)

The moon is half full. You're in the final stretch of the manifesting with the new moon cycle. This is the waning period as the moon decreases on its way to completing her cycle. The last quarter moon for every month is listed later within this section, as well as in the month-at-a-glance section.

This is a powerful time to take action on refining, adjusting and releasing. Breaking-free from negative thinking or worries is especially easy during this time as you flow with the pull from the waning moon.

Assess your progress. Identify any necessary changes. Release what is no longer supporting your manifesting desires.

This is a good time to discover if we've become out of sync somewhere. Notice any physical, emotional and spiritual imbalances. Maybe you're resenting giving so much time and energy into your dreams. Maybe you're losing confidence. Maybe you physically need some rest. This is the time to get refocused and re-establish balance. Investing in a fresh approach will infuse new energy and excitement into your new moon intention.

REFRESH

Investing in re-energizing yourself will invigorate your whole being. Here's a list of ways to perk your energy and your soul so you can assess your manifesting through a fresh lens.

- Get outdoors and appreciate the view.
- Call a friend and laugh. No business talk, just enjoying each other's company.
- Give yourself a hug
- Hug a pet
- Hug a friend
- Stretch
- Drink some water
- Eat chocolate
- Sing a song
- Dance
- Turn on lights. Better yet, get in the sunshine.
- Blow bubbles
- Skip
- Smell an orange or lemon
- Smile
- Breathe

THE DAY BEFORE NEXT NEW MOON

This is also referred to at the Dark Moon. It makes sense since the sky is dark. There's not even a glimmer of the moon. This is the easiest day of all.

Do nothing. Rest. Relax.

Moon Cycle Manifesting Guidesheet

This Moon Cycle Manifesting Guidesheet is also included as a full-sized printable. Please go to www.essentialmanifestingguidebook.com for your free download!

New Moon

New Moon is the initial time for manifesting. It's a time of foundation, new groundwork, new excitement, energy, and belief.

Each cycle is divided into 8-minute sections.

Set aside **8 minutes.**

STEP 1 – FOCUS

Set your timer for 30 seconds.

Relax. Remove distractions. Set your timer. Close your eyes and relax. As you relax for 1 minute bring your attention to one sound. When thoughts slip in, simply acknowledge them and return your attention to the sound. Release any tension through your body, especially your jaw, shoulders, hands and feet. Breathe.

STEP 2 – DECIDE

Set your timer for 2 minutes.

Decide 1–5 areas where you'd like new energy, new beginnings, new guidance, new starts, renewed strength. Consider the new moon's current astrological sign. Could you apply any of its specialties? Finish by asking yourself, "Is there anything else I'm ready to manifest at this time?" You may feel *nope, all good* or you may be surprised at the new insights revealed.

Here are some ideas to get you thinking.

new financial blessings	new projects
new clients	new social life
new love	new attitude
new exercise commitment	new excitement
renewed relationship	renewed strength
new self-care	new hope
new spiritual awakening	new ideas
new income	new home
new friendships	new car

STEP 3 – VISUALIZE

Set your timer for 2 minutes.

From your notes above, begin visualizing every desire you just wrote has manifested. Lean into the excitement, happiness, and joy of this manifested reality. Really feel the positive emotions. Smile, do a happy dance. Get into this celebration!

STEP 4 – AFFIRMATION

Set your timer for 2 minutes.

Write affirmations to support each of the desires manifested. Keep them positive and in the present tense. "Money constantly flows to me." Or "My body is healthy and whole."

You can also begin with "I am." For example, "I am loving my brand new convertible" or "I am a manifesting magnet."

STEP 5 – GRATITUDE

Set the timer for 30 seconds or skip the timer and go as long as you'd like.

Being grateful comes with a lot of health benefits. It also carries a lot of manifesting benefits. When you express your gratitude aloud you become a magnet for more things to be grateful for. Seriously. How cool is that?

You speak out thanking being grateful for this great day, having your dreams come true and your vibration just escalated on the manifesting scale. You are a noticeably beaming. A shining star. Then, you state your affirmation. It's positive, filled with present tense and you're offering gratitude for the affirmation you just stated. The universe hears you and is like, "Uh-oh, did I forget to give that to her? Eeeek! I've got to get right on that!"

When you're sharing your gratitude with the universe, be sure to include, "I'm so grateful for (this) or something better." Sometimes you underestimate the treasures that are just waiting for you to receive them. The "or something better" allows the "more" to come to you.

Know that what you've written has been added to the natural Law of Rhythm.

STEP 6 – EMBRACE

Set the timer for 1 minute.

Smile. Spend one minute feeling confident in your outcome.

For as the moon is illuminated so shall it be.

Moon Cycle Manifesting Guidesheet
Pg 179

New Moon -

8 minutes

Step 1 - Focus

Set your timer for 30 seconds.
Then, relax. Breathe. Relax even more.

Step 2 - Decide

Set your timer for 2 minutes.
Decide 1 - 5 areas where you'd like new energy, beginnings, renewed strength

- ☐ _____
- ☐ _____
- ☐ _____
- ☐ _____
- ☐ _____

Step 3- Visualize

Set your timer for 2 minutes.
Visualize your dream manifested. Go deep in the emotions. Celebrate

Step 4- Affirmation

Set your timer for 2 minutes.
Write affirmations to support each of the areas in Step 2.

- ☐ _____
- ☐ _____
- ☐ _____
- ☐ _____
- ☐ _____

New Moon Continued

Step 5 - Gratitude

Set your timer for 30 seconds.
Share your gratitude with the universe.
Remember this or something better!

Step 6 - Embrace

Set your timer for 1 minute.
Smile. Spend 1 minute. 60 seconds confident *knowing* this has manifested.

Write any intuitive messages.

_____

_____

_____

_____

_____

_____

_____

_____

_____

_____

First Quarter Moon

First Quarter Moon is the time for manifesting action steps.

Grab your New Moon Intention Worksheet and have it handy for this section.

STEP 1 – GROUND AND CENTER

Sit comfortably with feet flat on floor. Relax. Remove distractions. Set your timer. Close your eyes and relax. As you relax for 1 minute, bring your attention to one sound. When thoughts slip in, simply acknowledge them and return your attention to the sound. Release any tension through your body, especially your jaw, shoulders, hands and feet. Breathe.

STEP 2 – RECONNECT

Review your intentions, affirmations. What else can you be doing? Do you need blinders and earmuffs to tune out any negativity or distractions? Are you needing to jazz up your affirmations? Exhaustion and defeat can try to slip in so stay strong!

STEP 3 – RECOMMIT

Make a deal with yourself. At the top of your page write out your steps. Include this section at the bottom and sign and date.

> I, [name], commit to taking the action steps I intuitively know to take. I will say my affirmations daily. I will spend _____ time visualizing this has manifested. I will keep my thoughts focused on the outcome I desire and only on the outcome of this or something better manifested.
> Sign
> Date

Moon Cycle Manifesting Guidesheet

First Quarter Moon

Do this on 10th March

Step 1 - Ground and center

Relax. Breathe. Release any tension for at least 1 minute.

Step 2 - Reconnect

Review your intentions and affirmations. What steps can you take?

- [ ] _____
- [ ] _____
- [ ] _____
- [ ] _____
- [ ] _____

Step 3- Recommit

I _____, commit to taking the action steps I intuitively know to take.
I will say my affirmations daily. I will spend _____ time visualizing this
has manifested. I will keep my thoughts focused on the outcome I desire and
only on the outcome of this or something better manifested.

Sign _____

Date _____

Moon Cycle Plan

First Quarter _____   Date _____

Action steps

I will take this action

☐ _____   ☐ _____
☐ _____   ☐ _____
☐ _____   ☐ _____
☐ _____   ☐ _____
☐ _____   ☐ _____

Ideas to keep your manifesting vibration high and positive

Journaling   Energizing my water
Read my oracle cards   Applying chromotherapy
Work with spirit guides   Meditating
Smile   Commit to my affirmations

I will take this action

☐ _____   ☐ _____
☐ _____   ☐ _____

Think it. Speak it. Do it. Manifest it.

My Affirmation

┌───┐
│   │
│   │
│   │
│   │
└───┘

Full Moon

Large, bright, and round. This is invigorating. The full moon is offering total clarity on your new moon intentions.

Review Your New Moon Intention Sheet

Review your progress. Are any adjustments needed?

Physically – Take inventory of your actions. What's working? What isn't? What can you do to realign with your enthusiasm to this manifestation?

Emotionally – How are you feeling? Anxious? Bitter? Excited? Encouraged? Is there a theme your emotions are revealing?

Spiritually – Are you feeling the divine connection? Have you been trusting your intuition? This is a perfect opportunity to reconnect or strengthen the divine connection you already have.

Look over your general assessment of this month's progress. Take a cleansing breath as you see your paper. Don't let this be a time where you're beating yourself up. CELEBRATE everything you did right! I want hear the cheer even if you only said part of your affirmations. Cheer, even if you forgot all about your new moon intentions. Cheer that you woke up and shared your light with this world. This full moon is a time to fill with gratitude and let it overflow.

A special time of celebrations is cake and candles. You can make your own, buy one, or even skip the cake. Don't skip the candle though!

Grab a birthday candle. White, gold, pink, or blue are all great choices. Place in the cake or even hold it.

Prior to lighting, visualize your dream fulfilled. Imagine it has truly manifested. It feels so great doesn't it?

Any pings of negativity popping in? Any doubts? Could've or should'ves crossing your mind. That's okay.

Visualize your new moon intention manifested.

Light your candle.

You can sing this to the tune of Happy Birthday –

I am manifesting with the moon.
All my dreams do come true.
I have so much to celebrate....
I'm a manifestor, how 'bout you?

Blow out your candle. Safely dispose your candle and enjoy your cake! I know the song seems silly, but did you find yourself relaxing and maybe even smiling? That's the energy for manifesting! And, now you're doing it with the Moon Goddess joining you! How awesome is that?!

An aside... candles and cake dates back to Ancient Greece. A round cake (representing the moon) with candles on top were offered in celebration of the moon goddess, Artemis. The smoke from the candles would take the wishes, prayers and requests to the heavens. Talk about engaging with some additional manifesting help!

If cake and singing is not your cup of tea, here's a more conservative approach. No singing, but you can make up your own tune if you want!

Light your candle and state,

"I light this candle with the flame so bright.
Just like the moon, we are one with the light.
Dreams come true. I see it in my sight.
I manifest what I want and I know I am right."

Moon Cycle Plan

Full Moon in _____   My current time & day _____

Revelation, Fulfillment, Gratitude, Areas for change

My Full Moon celebration

Insights

_____

_____

_____

_____

_____

_____

_____

_____

Full Moon in _____   Date _____

I am so grateful for....

Insights

_____

_____

_____

_____

_____

_____

_____

_____

Moon Cycle Manifesting Guidesheet

Full Moon

Do a celebration that feels right to you. Dance in the moonlight? Read your cards? Make moon water? Something new?
(Refer to *The Essential Manifesting Guidebook 2022 pages 173, 183 and your Masterclass notes* for more ideas!

Once you've committed to a celebration or ritual please share it or comment in the Facebook Group. This brings energy to your intentions and manifesting! We are shining even brighter together!

I will....

- [ ] _____
- [ ] _____
- [ ] _____

Last Quarter Moon (also called Third Quarter)

The moon is half full. You're in the final stretch of the manifesting with the new moon cycle. This is the waning period as the moon decreases on its way to completing her cycle. The last quarter moon for every month is listed later within this section, as well as in the month-at-a-glance section.

This is one of my favorite times. It's like when you're doing a "spring cleaning" except it's with your cluttered thoughts, and action plans that have holes in them. You're emotionally and physically ready to toss them out.

This is usually that time when you're able to engage angels and be completely open to their ideas. This is where you really do embrace the "this or something better."

ANGEL TOOL

This has been one of the most powerful and magical manifesting tools for me, my children, friends, and clients. I really know this will be for you too!

On a fresh piece of paper draw a vertical line down the center of the page. Draw a horizontal line at the top of the page about 2 inches or 5 centimeters. This does not have to be perfect.

At the top of the left column write, "Angels." At the top of the right column write, "Me."

Write your angel to-do list. Write everything you want them to handle. Everything. All of your manifesting dreams. Those items from your New Moon Intention sheet goes in that angel column. Give it all to the angels.

For your column, write what you want to control. Items could include smiling, staying in the positive vibration, guarding your thoughts, and trusting your intuition. Remember, you are not to include the things you just gave to the angels.

When your list is complete, carry it around, place it at the side of your bed, take a photo and make it your wallpaper on your phone. It's important to not sneak in and take the manifesting duties from your angels. They've got this! And so do you!

Moon Cycle Plan

Third Quarter _____

Date _____

Last Quarter Moon (aka Third Quarter)

Step 1 - Review your New Moon intention.

> *Rewrite your New Moon intention here:*

What changes can you make? What can you release? Where can you open to new blessings, insights and even angel guidance? Be open and honest with yourself.

Step 2 - Revisit the current cosmic events and happenings. Go over your Masterclass notes and refer to your calendar and worksheets.

Current energies:

How can you apply these energies? Where will you implement in your manifesting?

Step 3 - Stay proactive and positive

You are in control. You have the power to manifest your dreams. Use this time to release or adjust what no longer works. Keep moving forward. Keep believing. Keep dreaming. You are closer than you realize.

ESSENTIAL MANIFESTING   WWW.SHINEANDALIGNWITHTRISH.COM   ©2023 TRISH MCKINNLEY, LLC

Third Quarter _____   Date _____

Adjustments to make. Things to release.

THOUGHTS	BODY	EMOTIONS
☐ _____	☐ _____	☐ _____
☐ _____	☐ _____	☐ _____
☐ _____	☐ _____	☐ _____
☐ _____	☐ _____	☐ _____
☐ _____	☐ _____	☐ _____

Gratitude enhances manifesting energy. List things you're grateful for in each category.

THOUGHTS	BODY	EMOTIONS
☐ _____	☐ _____	☐ _____
☐ _____	☐ _____	☐ _____
☐ _____	☐ _____	☐ _____
☐ _____	☐ _____	☐ _____
☐ _____	☐ _____	☐ _____

THE DAY BEFORE NEXT NEW MOON

This is also referred to at the Dark Moon. It makes sense since the sky is dark. There's not even a glimmer of the moon. This is the easiest day of all. Do nothing. Rest. Relax.

Right before New Moon

Step 1 - Cocoon in gratitude, confidence and peace.

All is well.

Step 2 - Explore self-care ideas.

Watch FB group for ideas, ask angels for guidance, trust your intuition. You know what is best for you and your manifesting energies at this time!

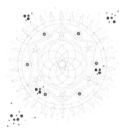

Before next New Moon

Rest. Relax. Revive your soul.

Commit to self-care during this time.

What will you do?

MIND

☐ _____

☐ _____

BODY

☐ _____

☐ _____

SOUL

☐ _____

☐ _____

Moon Magic & the Zodiac

Working with the lunar cycles, especially in alignment with the zodiac signs, is a practice rooted in ancient traditions. Harnessing the energy of the New Moon and Full Moon through the lens of the zodiac can provide a nuanced and powerful tool for manifestation and personal growth.

Here are some benefits of this practice:

1. Aligned Timing

New Moon: Traditionally seen as a time for new beginnings, intention setting, and planting seeds for future goals. When you understand the zodiac sign in which the New Moon occurs, you can tailor your intentions to align with the specific energies and themes of that sign.

Full Moon: Represents culmination, realization, and illumination. Knowing the zodiac sign of the Full Moon helps you focus on releasing or celebrating aspects related to that sign, aiding in letting go or expressing gratitude.

2. Focused Intentions

Each zodiac sign governs certain areas of life and has its unique energies. By understanding these, you can set more precise and resonant intentions. For instance:

- **Aries:** Initiatives, courage, and self-identity.
- **Taurus:** Material possessions, sensuality, and personal values.
- **Gemini:** Communication, learning, and adaptability.
- **Cancer:** Home, family, and emotional foundations.
- **Leo:** Self-expression, creativity, and heart-centered pursuits.
- **Virgo:** Daily routines, health, and acts of service.
- **Libra:** Relationships, balance, and harmony.
- **Scorpio:** Transformation, intimacy, and uncovering hidden truths.
- **Sagittarius:** Adventure, philosophy, and seeking higher truths.
- **Capricorn:** Ambition, career, and structures.
- **Aquarius:** Community, innovation, and humanitarian pursuits.
- **Pisces:** Intuition, dreams, and spiritual connections.

3. Deepened Self-Awareness

By aligning with the zodiac's energies during lunar events, you become more in tune with the cosmos's rhythms and, in turn, the rhythms within yourself. This deepened connection can enhance self-awareness and introspection.

4. Enhanced Manifestation Potential

Each zodiac sign carries specific energies that can amplify your manifestation efforts. For example, manifesting abundance during a Taurus New Moon (a sign associated with material wealth and stability) can be particularly potent.

5. Holistic Personal Growth

The zodiac offers a complete journey through various facets of the human experience. By working with each sign's lunar energies over the year, you engage in a comprehensive, holistic cycle of personal growth and development.

6. Reinforced Commitment

Having a monthly ritual aligned with the New and Full Moon keeps you consistently engaged with your personal growth journey. It acts as a regular checkpoint for reflection, intention-setting, and gratitude.

7. Connection to the Collective

Engaging in lunar practices linked to the zodiac can foster a sense of connection to the collective. Many people worldwide tune into these cosmic events, creating a collective consciousness focused on growth and transformation.

8. Energetic Cleansing and Renewal

The cyclical nature of the lunar phases, combined with the zodiac's archetypal energies, provides regular opportunities for energetic cleansing (during the waning phases) and renewal (during the waxing phases).

Aligning manifestation practices with the New Moon and Full Moon in the context of the zodiac signs provides a structured, nuanced, and powerful framework for personal growth, intention setting, and achieving desired outcomes in harmony with the cosmos.

It's kind of like the universe's secret. She's whispering, "Psssst! I know a shortcut!"

When you really vibe with the specific energies of each zodiac sign during the New and Full Moons, it is tapping into this awesome cosmic power. So, are you ready to be in the flow of the universe's rhythm and make your dreams feel supercharged?

SOME THINGS TO NOTE:

- Always check for the other cosmic events occurring during the New and Full Moon. your local times for the moon. If a new moon straddles a day, plant your new moon intentions on the day in your time zone or when you intuitively feel it is best for you.

- There are a couple moon events when retrogrades occur. Please jot these down for they are revealing.

- There are a couple supermoons. Please add these to your phone calendars and set reminders. These are powerful and fortuitous manifesting moments.

- There are several eclipses. Please, also add these to your schedule. These bring swift and successful manifesting change.

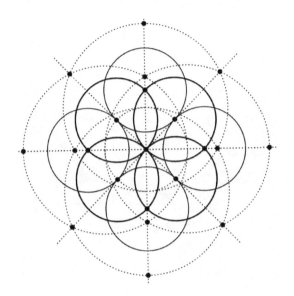

Cosmic spins, zodiac grins;
with every cycle, new magic
begins.

Moon in Aries

MANIFESTING ENERGIES: Initiatives, Courage, and Self-Identity

New Moon in Aries

New Moon in Aries Manifesting Tips

Oh, the New Moon in Aries! It's like lighting a matchstick in a starlit realm. Imagine starting a race with an extra boost or launching a rocket with additional fuel—that's the zesty and invigorating energy Aries brings to the New Moon's typical 'fresh start' vibes. Aries, being the first sign of the zodiac, infuses this moon phase with a pioneering spirit, making it a prime time to kickstart new projects or breathe fiery life into dormant dreams. If you've been waiting for that cosmic nudge to jumpstart your desires, this moon's your magical catapult. The universe is not just whispering, but shouting, "Go for it!"

New Moon in Aries Ritual

Reclaiming the Warrior Within Ritual

Harness the bold and initiating energy of Aries to reclaim one's personal power, standing strong in one's true essence.

MATERIALS:

- A large mirror although a small mirror will do (to reflect your inner warrior)
- A red cloth or scarf (symbolizing Aries' passionate energy)
- A bowl of water with a pinch of salt (for cleansing)
- A piece of paper and pen
- A strong, grounding stone, like hematite or black tourmaline

DIRECTIONS:

Start by clearing your ritual space mentally. Envision a protective circle around you, ensuring only positive energies can enter.

Have your salt water and writing tools nearby.

Stand in front of the mirror or hold the mirror in front of you. Look deeply into your eyes and recognize the warrior within, waiting to be re-awakened. Breathe deeply and connect with this powerful aspect of yourself.

Write down on the paper an affirmation that resonates with reclaiming your power. For instance, *"I am strong, capable, and in control of my destiny."* Hold this written affirmation close to your heart and take a few moments to feel its truth.

Dip your fingers into the salted water. Touch your forehead, heart, and both wrists, imagining any energy blocks or ties holding you back dissolving away. As you do this, say:

> *"With every touch, I cleanse and clear,*
> *Reclaiming my power, I hold dear."*

Hold grounding stone in your hands, allowing its stabilizing energy to fortify your resolve. Visualize a strong, unshakeable foundation being formed within you. Place the stone on top of your written affirmation, grounding your intention.

Drape the red cloth or scarf around your shoulders like a warrior's cape. Feel its warm energy enveloping you, enhancing your sense of power and confidence.

Stand tall, feet slightly apart in a grounded stance, like Wonder Woman or your favorite superhero. Breathe deeply, drawing energy from the earth and the cosmos. Feel a surge of power rising within you with each breath.

When ready, state your affirmation. Repeat it out loud three times, putting emphasis and belief into each word. Allow the energy of your words to permeate your being.

Fold the paper and place it with the grounding stone in a safe space, like a personal altar or a drawer, as a reminder of your reclaimed power. Thank the energies of Aries and your inner warrior for their guidance and strength.

This ritual taps into the fearless Aries energy to help you reconnect with and reclaim your personal power.

You may be thinking I just want to manifest more money, losing these extra pounds, or that special love. I get it. That's why this ritual is the very first New Moon ritual. Reclaiming your personal power is integral to the manifestation process.

Imagine your personal power as this radiant, pulsating energy, kind of like a magical core within you. When it's strong and glowing, it's like having a supercharged magnet, drawing in all the things you're manifesting with ease and clarity. It's that confident stride of a lion, knowing it rules its world. Now, let's break it down:

1. **Clarity of Intent:** By reclaiming your power, you get to know your true self better. You understand what you genuinely want, not just what others want for you or what society expects. It's like having a compass that always points to your true north, your heart's deepest desires.

2. **Boosted Confidence:** Think of it as having a magic wand that you're sure will work. When you trust in your power and abilities, you emit this confident vibe. This energy acts like a beacon, signaling the universe that you're ready to receive what you've asked for.

3. **Eliminating Limiting Beliefs:** Reclaiming personal power often means shedding those pesky, limiting beliefs that act like boulders blocking your path. Without these blocks, the road to manifesting becomes a smooth, downhill ride.

4. **Increased Resilience:** Even in magic, things don't always go as planned. With strong personal power, setbacks become mere detours. You'll have the strength to bounce back, adjust, and continue on your manifesting journey.

5. **Alignment with the Universe:** At its core, personal power aligns you with the universe's flow. When you're in sync, you become this conduit for manifesting magic. It's like dancing harmoniously with the cosmos, and in that dance, all you desire comes flowing effortlessly to you.

In essence, reclaiming your personal power supercharges your manifestation abilities. It's like whispering into the universe's ear and knowing it's listening intently, ready to grant your wishes. So, darling manifestor, wear that crown of personal power, wave your wand, and let the magic unfold!

Full Moon In Aries

Full Moon in Aries Manifesting Tips

Alright, dive in with me for a sec: Picture you're on the starting line of a grand cosmic race, fire in your belly and the wind teasing at your hair. That electrifying sensation? That's the Full Moon in Aries at work! This moon phase is like a celestial power-up, charging you with energy, courage, and a hint of daring. Aries, with its fiery spirit and trailblazing leadership, transforms this Full Moon into a beacon for taking decisive action and chasing after your passions with renewed gusto. It's the universe nudging you and saying, "Hey, remember those dreams? It's time to make them happen!" Whether it's taking the lead on a project, bravely pursuing a new path, or simply igniting the spark of a long-held desire, the Full Moon in Aries is your cosmic cheerleader, urging you on with a fiery pep in your step. Lace up those cosmic sneakers and sprint towards your destiny!

Full Moon in Aries Ritual

Fire-Passion Ignition

PURPOSE: To kindle your desires, reigniting passions, and fueling the determination to chase after your dreams.

MATERIALS:

- A small red candle (symbolizing Aries' fiery nature)
- A bowl of water (for safety and to contrast the fire with the watery energy of the moon)
- Pen and paper
- Matches or a lighter
- A pinch of cinnamon or ginger (optional, for added fire energy)

DIRECTIONS:

Find a quiet space where you won't be disturbed. If possible, sit where you can see the moon, feeling its powerful glow. If you want, play some uplifting or motivational music softly in the background.

Place your bowl of water nearby as a safety measure. Sprinkle your candle with the pinch of cinnamon or ginger, if using. This adds an extra kick of fiery energy!

Think of a goal, desire, or intention that fills you with passion—something you're burning to achieve. Write it down on the paper, pouring all your fiery Aries energy into each word.

When that feels complete, light your candle. As you light the candle, say aloud, *"With the fire of Aries and the glow of the Full Moon, I ignite my desires and set my intentions aflame!"*

Spend a few minutes looking into the candle's flame, visualizing your dreams coming to life. Watch the flame dance. Let the warm energy fill you up, amplifying your determination and drive.

Once you feel your energy charged and your intentions set, blow out the candle, imagining your desires being carried into the universe with the smoke. Dip your fingers into the bowl of water, and lightly sprinkle some on the paper with your intention, symbolizing the harmony of fire and water in your ritual.

Conclude by saying, *"By the power of Aries and the Full Moon, may my desires be fueled, and my path be clear."*

Store the paper in a special place, such as a sacred box, journal, or altar. Periodically charge your intentions, using the paper as a tangible reminder of what you're manifesting.

Charging your intention paper amplifies its energy, creating a stronger vibrational alignment with your goals. Here are several methods to energetically charge your intention paper while you await its manifestation:

1. **Moonlight Bath:** Place your intention paper under the moonlight, especially during a New Moon (for beginnings) or Full Moon (for culmination). The moon's energies amplifies the potency of your intentions.

2. **Crystals:** Certain crystals, like clear quartz (universal amplifier), malachite (for abundance), or rose quartz (for love), can be used

to charge your intention paper. Lay the crystal on top of or around the paper, visualizing its energy infusing the paper.

3. **Meditation:** Hold the intention paper close to your heart or third-eye chakra while meditating. Visualize your intention manifesting and feel the emotions associated with its realization.

4. **Sacred Space:** Keep the intention paper on a personal altar or sacred space. The energy of this space, combined with other spiritually significant items, can charge the paper continuously.

5. **Sunlight:** Just as moonlight charges with feminine, receptive energy, sunlight imbues with active, masculine energy. A few hours of sun exposure can charge the intention paper with radiant, manifesting energy.

6. **Elements:** Introduce the paper to the four elements. Pass it briefly over a candle flame (fire), sprinkle it with water or let it absorb morning dew (water), allow it to catch wind breezes (air), and place it upon soil or salt (earth).

7. **Aromatherapy:** Infuse the paper with essential oils aligned with your intention. For example, lavender for peace, cinnamon for attraction, or patchouli for grounding. Dab a few drops on the paper or keep it in a sachet with herbs.

8. **Mantras and Affirmations:** Speak or chant mantras or affirmations over the paper, verbalizing your commitment to your intention and asking the universe for its support.

9. **Visualization:** Daily, take a moment to focus on the paper, visualizing a beam of light entering it and charging your intention with universal energy.

10. **Energy Work:** If you're familiar with Reiki, Qi Gong, or my energy ball method, channel this energy into the paper, visualizing it glowing with amplified vibrancy.

11. **Sacred Geometry:** Place the paper within geometric patterns like the Flower of Life or under a pyramid shape. These structures are believed to resonate with cosmic energies and can amplify your intention's vibrancy.

12. **Sound Healing:** Use tuning forks, singing bowls, or even uplifting music to bathe the paper in sound waves, raising its vibrational frequency.

The most important aspect is your intention and belief. Trust in the process and feel confident in the energetic charge you're providing to your written goals. This trust and confidence, combined with the methods above, will strengthen the manifestation process.

This Full Moon in Aries ritual is a potent blend of fiery intent and moonlit promise. It's designed to be simple yet impactful, perfect for setting your sights high and charging towards your goals with renewed zest. Happy manifesting!

Flower of Life

The Flower of Life is a universal symbol, representing the cycle of creation, encompassing life, consciousness, and existence. It's believed to contain the patterns of creation as they emerged from the Great Void.

Just as the circles interlock and overlap, the Flower of Life signifies the interconnectedness of all life and spirits in the universe. It showcases that everything is connected and originates from a single source.

The Flower of Life symbol can be found around the world, everywhere, from Egyptian temples to Japanese shrines. Its widespread presence indicates its universal importance and recognition across cultures and eras

Bottom line: The Flower of Life isn't just some random doodle; it's like the universe's brand logo, reminding us of the big cosmic party we're all a part of. So, next time you spot it, give a nod to the universe's rad design skills!

Moon in Taurus

MANIFESTING ENERGIES: Material Possessions, Sensuality, and Personal Values.

New Moon in Taurus

New Moon in Taurus Manifesting Tips

Alright, picture this: You're standing at the edge of a lush, untouched field, the soil rich and teeming with potential. That's the essence of the New Moon in Taurus for you! It's like the universe hands you a golden trowel and whispers, "The ground is ripe, start planting!" Taurus, with its earthly magic and a knack for growth, makes this New Moon the ideal time to sow the seeds of your most treasured dreams. It's not just about dreaming big, but grounding those dreams in reality, laying down solid roots.

This moon phase beckons you to embrace patience and perseverance, to nurture your intentions with care and consistency. So, when you're setting your sights on future abundance, know that the New Moon in Taurus is the cosmic fertilizer, giving your aspirations the nourishment they need to flourish and thrive. Time to get your hands a little dirty and watch the magic sprout!

New Moon in Taurus Ritual

Prosperity Pouch Creation

PURPOSE: To create a talisman of wealth and abundance, charging it with Taurus energy under the New Moon.

MATERIALS:

- A small green or gold pouch or piece of cloth and string
- Coins (preferably shiny or special ones you're drawn to)
- A small piece of paper and a pen
- Cinnamon (for attraction and abundance)
- A crystal like green aventurine, citrine, or jade (associated with prosperity)

DIRECTIONS:

Find a quiet and comfortable space, perhaps decorated with earth-toned colors. Play some gentle, grounding music.

On the piece of paper, jot down the amount of money you'd like to manifest or a specific financial goal. Fold the paper into a small size.

Open up your pouch or lay out your piece of cloth. Place your folded intention inside.

Add the coins, saying, *"With each coin, my wealth grows."* Sprinkle a pinch of cinnamon, saying, *"With this spice, I attract prosperity and abundance."* Lastly, add the crystal, affirming, *"With this stone, my financial endeavors are charged and amplified."*

Draw the pouch closed or, if using a cloth, gather the edges and tie it up with the string. Hold the sealed pouch in both hands, visualizing it glowing with a green or golden light, brimming with prosperous energy.

Say aloud, *"Under this New Moon in Taurus, I harness the energies of growth, stability, and abundance. May this pouch amplify my financial intentions and draw prosperity into my life."*

Sleep with the prosperity pouch under your pillow for the first night. After that, keep it in your purse, wallet, or a special place in your home. Whenever you touch or see the pouch, remember your financial intentions and feel the abundant energies it holds.

This ritual takes advantage of tactile items and Taurus's penchant for material manifestations.

The act of physically creating and holding your prosperity pouch can serve as a powerful reminder of your intentions and the wealth you aim to draw into your life.

The prosperity pouch you've created is a talisman infused with your intentions, and as with most items, its treatment is largely based on your personal feelings and intuition. However, here are some general guidelines and suggestions:

1. Regularly Recharge: Every New and Full Moon (or specifically during a Taurus Moon for added potency), you can reopen the pouch, review your intention, and recharge it with fresh energy. This can be done by holding the pouch under moonlight, meditating with it, or even adding a fresh coin, crystal or sprinkle of cinnamon.

2. Achieving Your Goal: Once you've achieved your financial goal or manifestation, you can choose to:

   • Disassemble and Thank: Open the pouch, thank each item for its role, and then return the materials to the Earth or use them in other rituals.

   • Repurpose: Keep the pouch but rewrite a new intention to keep the prosperity energy flowing and adapt to your new goals.

- Store the pouch in a sacred space as a reminder of your manifestation prowess.

3. If over time you feel the pouch's energy has diminished or if you've outgrown its purpose:

   - Cleanse and Restart: Cleanse the items (perhaps using sage smoke or moonlight), set a new intention, and begin the process anew.

   - Return to Nature: As a gesture of gratitude, you might bury the pouch or its contents in the Earth, symbolizing the completion of one cycle and the potential beginning of another.

4. On an annual basis, or during significant life changes, revisit the pouch. Reflect on your financial journey, and decide if the pouch still aligns with your goals and intentions. Adjust as needed.

Remember, the most important aspect of any ritual or talisman is the intention and energy you infuse into it. The pouch is an external representation of your inner desires and commitment to your goals. Treat it with respect and gratitude, and let it serve as a tool on your manifestation journey.

Enjoy your journey toward abundant prosperity!

Full Moon in Taurus

Full Moon in Taurus Manifesting Tips

Imagine for a moment you're stepping into the most luxurious garden, where every flower is in full bloom and the scent of rich earth and blossoms envelops you. That's the vibe of the Full Moon in Taurus! This moon phase is like nature's most opulent embrace, grounding you deeply while illuminating your senses. Taurus, with its Earthy strength and

Venus-ruled love for beauty and abundance, makes this Full Moon perfect for manifesting tangible and lasting results. Think of it as the universe's green light for turning your dreams into something you can touch, see, and feel. Whether you're looking to bring more stability, nurture your self-worth, or manifest something deliciously decadent, the Full Moon in Taurus is all about savoring the journey and reaping the rewards. So, under this moonlight, go ahead and plant those seeds of desire, knowing they're destined to grow into the most sumptuous fruits!

Full Moon in Taurus Ritual

The Full Moon Abundance Dance

MATERIALS:

- A space where you can move freely under the moonlight (a backyard, patio, or even an open window with a view of the moon).
- Comfortable clothing.
- A small crystal or gemstone (like rose quartz or citrine).
- Your favorite uplifting music (have playlist ready).
- A piece of paper and a pen.

DIRECTIONS:

1. Choose a clear night when the Full Moon is visible. Step outside and create a cozy, sacred space. You can light a few candles, set up some cushions, or create a circle with stones or flowers.

2. Start by smudging your space with sage or palo santo. Imagine the smoke clearing away any negative energy, leaving only room for positive vibes.

3. Wear comfortable clothing that makes you feel abundant and confident. Adorn yourself with your chosen crystal or gemstone, which will be your manifesting partner.

4. Take a moment to write down your intentions or desires on the piece of paper. Be clear and specific about what you want to manifest. Fold the paper and hold it in your hand.

5. Stand under the moonlight, holding the folded paper and your crystal. Close your eyes, take a few deep breaths, and imagine your intentions coming to life. Visualize yourself living your desired reality, feeling the emotions associated with achieving your goals. Stay in this space until you're ready to celebrate.

6. Put on your favorite music, preferably something rhythmic and joyful. Begin to dance freely and energetically. Imagine that with every move, you are attracting abundance and bringing your intentions closer to manifestation. Let the energy flow through you.

7. Hold your crystal high above your head and say, "*I charge this crystal under the Full Moon's abundance light to amplify my intentions and manifest my desires.*" Hold it up to the moon for a few moments, feeling the moon's energy infusing it.

8. When you're ready, sit down and release your intentions to the universe. Burn the folded paper with a candle or safely dispose of it as a symbol of surrendering your desires to the cosmos.

9. Close the ritual with a short gratitude meditation. Express thanks for the abundance you already have in your life and for the manifestations on their way.

10. Enjoy a small treat like a piece of dark chocolate or a glass of wine as you soak in the moonlight, celebrating your manifesting dance.

11. When you're done, thank the moon for her energy and the universe for listening to your intentions. Blow out any candles, and go to bed feeling grateful and abundant.

Manifesting with the Bull Power Animal: Unleash the Power Within

The bull, a symbol of raw power, steadfastness, and prosperity, offers unique energies to bolster your manifestation journey. When you align with the bull as your power animal, you're embracing a potent ally that will supercharge your intentions and desires.

Manifesting with the bull encourages perseverance. Even when faced with setbacks or slow progress, the bull's spirit compels you to stay on course, ensuring that you hold onto your vision with an iron grip until it materializes.

The sheer physical strength of the bull translates to a significant energetic boost when manifesting. This means not only setting intentions but charging towards them with immense vigor, breaking down any barriers that stand in your way. By manifesting with its energy, you amplify your ability to attract wealth, success, and abundance in all its forms.

To manifest with the bull power animal is to tap into an age-old reservoir of power, determination, and abundance. By understanding and harnessing these benefits, you're poised to manifest your desires with an unmatched potency. So, envision that powerful bull by your side, and watch as your intentions manifest into reality.

Moon in Gemini

MANIFESTING ENERGIES: Communication,
Learning, and Adaptability.

New Moon in Gemini

New Moon in Gemini Manifesting Tips

Imagine the night sky as a vast cosmic chat room, and when the Full Moon hangs out in chatty Gemini, it's like the universe is buzzing with a thousand conversations. Gemini's airy and communicative vibes make this moon phase a prime time for brainstorming and verbalizing your dreams. Think of it as the universe being super receptive to every thought, whisper, and shout of your desires.

When manifesting during this Full Moon in Gemini, it's not just about feeling your wishes, but voicing them, making them known, and watching them echo across the cosmic realms. So, during this energetic time, grab a buddy, have a heart-to-heart under the moonlight, and let your intentions fly on the wings of Gemini's twin energy. It's all about doubling the magic, amplifying your voice, and believing that if one door closes, a universe of possibilities still beckons!

New Moon in Gemini Ritual

Tapping into Gemini's communicative strength, writing down paired intentions that resonate with both your head and heart.

MATERIALS:

- A notebook or two pieces of paper
- A pen or two different colored pens
- Incense or sage for cleansing (optional)
- Crystals like clear quartz or moonstone (optional, for amplifying intentions)
- Soft background music or sounds (like wind chimes or birdsong)

DIRECTIONS:

Begin by purifying your space. Light your incense or sage and let the smoke waft around you, clearing away any stagnant energies and making room for fresh intentions.

Embracing Gemini's twin nature, decide on two primary areas or themes you want to focus on. This could be things like 'Career & Health', 'Love & Self-growth', 'Adventure & Learning' – any two areas that speak to you.

On one page or piece of paper, write down your intentions related to the first theme. On the opposite page or other paper, jot down intentions for the second theme. Using two different colored pens can make this process visually delightful and help separate the energies.

Holding your notebook or papers close, close your eyes and imagine the New Moon's silvery light showering down on you, illuminating your intentions and making them radiant with possibilities.

If you're using crystals, place them on top of your written intentions, visualizing them boosting the energy of your dreams and desires.

Sit for a few moments in silent gratitude. As Gemini rules communication, you might even whisper a 'Thank You' to the universe, ensuring your intentions are heard.

Store your notebook or papers in a sacred space, perhaps by a window or on an altar. As the moon waxes, let it be a reminder of the seeds you've planted, ready to grow and flourish.

Each time you revisit your intentions, you'll be reminded of the fresh start and infinite possibilities the New Moon in Gemini offers.

Full Moon in Gemini

Full Moon in Gemini Manifesting Tips

Okay, let's dive into the cosmic dance of the Full Moon in Gemini! Imagine the night sky as a vast cosmic chat room, and when the Full Moon hangs out in chatty Gemini, it's like the universe is buzzing with a thousand conversations. Gemini's airy and communicative vibes make this moon phase a prime time for brainstorming and verbalizing your dreams. Think of it as the universe being super receptive to every thought, whisper, and shout of your desires.

When manifesting during this Full Moon in Gemini, it's not just about feeling your wishes, but voicing them, making them known, and watching them echo across the cosmic realms. So, during this energetic time, grab a buddy, have a heart-to-heart under the moonlight, and let your intentions fly on the wings of Gemini's twin energy. It's all about doubling the magic, amplifying your voice, and believing that if one door closes, a universe of possibilities still beckons!

Full Moon in Gemini Ritual

To illuminate your intentions, letting them shine brightly with the energy of Gemini.

MATERIALS:

- Two lanterns (paper or metal, preferably the kind that can be hung or placed on a surface rather than released into the air)
- LED tea lights or battery-operated candles (for safety and reusability)
- Permanent markers
- A piece of paper and a pen

DIRECTIONS:

1. Choose a clear outdoor space or a well-ventilated indoor area where you can view or feel the Full Moon's energy.

2. On your piece of paper, jot down two desires or intentions you wish to manifest, embracing Gemini's dual nature.

3. Take each paper lantern and, with your permanent marker, inscribe a keyword or symbol representing each intention onto them.

4. With the lanterns in front of you, close your eyes and visualize your intentions coming to life, amplified by the Full Moon in Gemini's radiance.

5. Place an LED tea light or battery-operated candle inside each lantern. As you turn them on, imagine the light as a beacon for your wishes, signaling to the universe.

6. Sit with your illuminated lanterns, feeling the warmth and glow of your intentions. Thank the Full Moon and Gemini for their guiding and communicative energies.

7. Store the lanterns in a special place, and over time, light them during moments of reflection or when you wish to revisit your intentions.

The lanterns act as a lasting reminder of your intentions, ready to shine any time you need them!

Cancer

Moon in Cancer

MANIFESTING ENERGIES: Home, Family,
and Emotional Foundations

New Moon in Cancer

New Moon in Cancer Manifesting Tips

Alright, picture this: The New Moon in Cancer is like that moment when you find the coziest spot in your home, wrap yourself in a plush blanket, and get ready to journal your dreams. It's all about diving deep into your emotional realm, where wishes aren't just fleeting thoughts but come straight from the heart's core.

This moon phase, with Cancer's motherly and intuitive touch, acts as a celestial whisper, nudging you to listen to your innermost desires. When you manifest under this lunar embrace, it's like the universe becomes a caring confidant, holding space for your most tender aspirations. So, harness this energy by pouring a cup of moonlit tea, sinking into your feelings, and letting your dreams flow, knowing they're being cradled in the universe's loving arms.

New Moon in Cancer Ritual

1. Set your intention for peace, tranquility, and relaxation to flow. Add any new moon intentions you already created.

2. Make a cup of your favorite tea.

3. As the tea is steeping in your mug, cradle the mug between your fingers as if cherishing the mug and the contents within.

4. Close your eyes.

5. Imagine sparkles of love, light, and the manifesting energies that you desire showering into the mug. (For example: areas you want freedom, clear communication with family, obvious intuitive insight, better relationships)

6. When you feel your tea is charged with your desires, say,

   "Thank you for the blessings flowing and imbued into this tea. I gratefully receive all the energetic gifts as it becomes a part of me."

7. Sip the tea and leisurely enjoy allowing the increased vibration to do its thing!

Full Moon in Cancer

Full Moon in Cancer Manifesting Tips

Oh, honey, when the Full Moon cozies up in the nurturing embrace of Cancer, it's like the universe is inviting you over for a heartfelt chat over cups of moonlit tea. This lunar phase, wrapped in Cancer's intuitive and tender vibes, amplifies our emotional and intuitive powers. It's the time when the universe is all ears, listening intently to the deepest desires of your heart. Manifesting under this moon isn't just about visualizing goals—it's about pouring your very soul into them.

Cancer encourages you to connect with your emotions, making your intentions resonate on a deeply personal level. So, with the Full Moon in Cancer, think of it as manifesting with soulful magic. Your desires aren't just wishes; they're profound emotional connections that the universe is eager to nurture and bring to life. It's pure celestial magic, wrapped in a warm, comforting blanket!

Full Moon in Cancer Ritual

Channel the emotional and intuitive energy of Cancer, capturing your dreams and memories under the Full Moon's glow.

MATERIALS:

- A clear glass jar with a lid
- Moonlit water (water left under the moonlight for a night)
- Small shells or sea stones (representing Cancer, the crab)
- Slips of paper and a pen
- A tealight or small candle
- Lavender or chamomile essential oil (optional, for added relaxation)

DIRECTIONS:

Choose a quiet, cozy spot where you can sit comfortably. Light the tealight or candle and set it near your setup. If using essential oil, dab a little on your wrists to create a calming ambiance.

On the slips of paper, jot down memories you're grateful for and dreams you'd like to manifest. These can be feelings, experiences, or anything that resonates with you.

Begin by placing a few shells or sea stones at the base of the jar. As you add each one, think of a foundation you're building upon - your past experiences that have shaped you.

Pour the moonlit water into the jar, imagining it as the Full Moon's energy amplifying your intentions.

Fold your slips of paper and place them gently into the water-filled jar. As each slip submerges, imagine it absorbing the moon's energy and activating its manifestation magic.

Hold the jar close to your heart and express gratitude for past experiences and hope for the dreams you've set into motion. Visualize them coming to life in the nurturing energy of Cancer and say, *"By the gentle glow of the moon and the nurturing embrace of Cancer's tide, I give thanks for memories past and dreams yet to arrive. To the universe, so vast and wide, I send my gratitude for being my guide. With every ebb and flow inside, my heart and soul are amplified. Blessed be this moment, where gratitude and magic reside."* Feel free to adapt this blessing to resonate more personally with you.

Close the jar's lid, sealing in the magic. Blow out the candle, imagining the smoke carrying your intentions to the universe.

If possible, leave the jar out under the moonlight overnight to charge further. Otherwise, place it somewhere special to you.

This ritual encapsulates the nurturing energy of Cancer and the transformative power of the Full Moon. As the days progress, you can look at your jar as a reminder of your powerful intentions and the deep emotional currents propelling them forward. It's like having a little bottle of moonlit ocean magic, teeming with memories and dreams!

Moon in Leo

MANIFESTING ENERGIES: Self-expression, Creativity, and Heart-Centered Pursuits

New Moon in Leo

New Moon in Leo Manifesting Tips

Think of this lunar phase as a cosmic backstage, where you're prepping for the grandest show of your life. The New Moon's fresh-start vibes, combined with Leo's fiery passion, gives you this incredible energy to dream big and set the stage for some show-stopping manifestations. It's all about heart-driven intentions during this time. Leo encourages you to tap into what sets your soul on fire, igniting desires that resonate with your true essence. So, as you manifest under this New Moon in Leo, you're not just wishing—you're putting out a royal decree to the universe, ready to take the lead role in the beautiful play of your life. With Leo's confidence and the New Moon's magic, the spotlight's on you, and darling, you're born to shine!

New Moon in Leo Ritual

MATERIALS:

- a gold plate;
- crystals to represent the sun: sunstone, pyrite, tigers eye, citrine.
- Sunflowers, daisies or any gold/yellow flowers, as well as any flowers that make you feel sexy and celebrated.
- Essential oils like orange, lemon, bergamot, and amber.
- Diffuser or cork for essential oil application.
- Three gold or yellow candles.
- Matches.
- Any other items that you feel represent the sun.
- Hair mask or apply this Leo DIY ¼ cup honey, ½ cup organic coconut oil, 4 Tbs cinnamon. Blend together and adjust any ingredient amounts for your hair's thickness and length. You can always test a section of your hair prior or simply substitute your conditioner.
- Towel – white, yellow or gold.
- Grab paper or canvas, paints, markers, colored pencils (including gold).

DIRECTIONS:

In your prepared sacred space have all of your supplies.

Set your art supplies (paints, markers, canvas, paper), flowers and essential oils on a table in a comfortable spot. This is where you'll be doing the creative step. If you have essential oils, add to your diffuser or dab some of your oil on cork. Place by the flowers.

Take a moment a connect with the beauty you've created.

Add the gold plate to your table away from your flowers. Place the candles in the center on your gold plate. As you light your candles say, *"I welcome the energy of the sun, the lion and the new moon."*

Add the crystals to the outside of the candles to represent the rays of sunshine. As you place say, *"With each crystal, I tune into and harmonize with this warm, loving, New Moon in Leo energies."*

Take a cleansing breath and apply your hair mask saying, *"I celebrate, enhance and strengthen my sexy, strong lioness (or lion's) mane."*

Wrap the towel around your hair.

Using your art supplies, draw, paint or sketch whatever the new moon energies reveal. Allow your creativity to flow. No editing or judging. Whatever you are creating is perfect! When you feel your art is complete, take a moment and write three new moon intentions on your paper.

When finished, put away your art supplies and let your canvas dry.

Prior to extinguishing the candles state your new moon intentions. Right before blowing out the candles say, *"I gratefully send these new moon intentions into the air. From my breath they are set into motion. Guided in the wind by the goddess, the angels and the lion and taken to manifesting fulfillment by the light of the moon. And, it is so."*

Extinguish the candles. If you're able, leave all of this set in your sacred space and come back to during this moon's cycle for recharging.

Wash your hair and then take the time for self-care. Leo loves pampering and self-care. Spend the rest of the day celebrating you and your dreams. You'll find the manifesting doors opening with the warmth and love of the sun.

Full Moon in Leo

Full Moon in Leo Manifesting Tips

Alright, so imagine the Full Moon draped in a regal cloak of shimmering gold, radiating the kind of confidence that only Leo can flaunt. When the Full Moon struts into Leo, it's like the universe's spotlight is beaming directly onto your grandest dreams and most heartfelt desires. This is the time to embrace your inner star and let your passions take center stage. Leo's fiery energy, combined with the illuminating glow of the Full Moon, creates a celestial stage perfect for manifesting dreams that align with your truest self and heart's calling. So, during this moon phase, think big, love deeply, and let your intentions roar with confidence, because the universe is totally applauding your performance!

Full Moon in Leo Ritual

MATERIALS:

- A gold or yellow candle (representing Leo's sunny and royal energy)
- A piece of paper and a bold pen or marker
- A small crown or tiara (optional, but adds to the fun!)
- A bowl or dish
- Glitter or gold sequins (optional, for added sparkle)

DIRECTIONS:

Clean and set your space, placing the gold or yellow candle in the center of your chosen area.

If you have a tiara or crown, place it upon your head. Embrace that Leo confidence! Feel yourself as the ruler of your destiny.

On the piece of paper, write a bold declaration of what you're aiming to manifest. Make it grand, just like a royal decree. For example: *"By the power of this Leo Full Moon, I declare abundance in all aspects of my life!"*

If you're using glitter or gold sequins, sprinkle some around your written declaration. Let it represent the shimmering energy of your intentions.

As you light the candle, imagine its flame as the roaring fire of Leo's heart, burning away any doubts and amplifying your desires.

Hold your paper to your heart, then read your declaration out loud with confidence and flair. Imagine the Full Moon's light casting a spotlight on you, magnifying your intentions to the universe.

Place the piece of paper in the bowl or dish and position it where it can bask under the moonlight. If possible, leave it overnight to charge.

Express gratitude to the Full Moon in Leo for its empowering energy. Feel the warmth and courage filling your heart.

Once you feel your intentions have been set and acknowledged by the universe, blow out the candle, imagining your dreams being carried by the smoke to the cosmos.

Afterwards, store your paper in a safe space.

This Full Moon in Leo ritual captures the essence of Leo's boldness and the Full Moon's magnifying power. By declaring your dreams with authority and style, you're not just manifesting, but also celebrating your inner royalty and potential. Shine on and let your intentions roar!

Connect with Leo energy by letting your hair be rather wild. Wear gold jewelry.

Standing in front of a mirror, begin looking at yourself. Really look at yourself through the eyes of love. Begin complimenting yourself. Leos love receiving and giving compliments. State these compliments aloud. This full moon energy is revealing all of your great qualities.

Place your hands on your hips, striking a power pose. Share in the mirror tales of your success, great qualities, and natural awesomeness.

Spend five minutes doing this activity in front of your mirror complimenting yourself the whole time. No meanness or sharing of disappointments. This is a time of positivity, love, and celebration.

Next, tell the mirror of your manifesting dreams except state as they have already manifested. Share the story of how it happened. Share the joy, the gratitude, and the celebration.

When you feel complete, look in the mirror and say, "I love you! You are purrfect just the way you are!"

Let the sexiness and power continue to flow! Feel free to do this ritual any time you need a boost of Leo confidence and courage.

Power Pose

Moon in Virgo

MANIFESTING ENERGIES: Daily Routines,
Health, and Acts of Service

New Moon in Virgo

New Moon in Virgo Manifesting Tips

Oh, let me tell you about the magic of the New Moon in Virgo! Picture this: It's like having your very own celestial life coach who's armed with a magic wand and an impeccably detailed planner. The New Moon is all about fresh starts, right? Now, combine that with Virgo's knack for precision and a touch of earthy magic, and what you get is the perfect moment to plant your intentions with clarity.

Virgo helps you get specific, making sure your dreams aren't just whimsical but are also grounded and actionable. So, when you're manifesting under this New Moon, it's not just about casting wishes to the stars—it's about weaving magic into the very fabric of your day-to-day life. Dream big, but also remember, Virgo's energy is cheering you on to map out the baby steps to get there!

New Moon in Virgo Ritual

Utilize the New Moon's energy in Virgo, a sign ruled by Mercury, to set clear intentions through reflection and affirmation.

MATERIALS:

- A handheld mirror or a larger mirror you can gaze into
- A white or silver candle
- Lavender or eucalyptus essential oil (optional)
- A piece of paper and a pen

DIRECTIONS:

Find a quiet space, preferably tidy (embracing that Virgo energy!). Light the candle and set it near your mirror. If you're using essential oil, dab a tiny bit on your wrists and temples to clear your mind.

Holding the mirror or gazing into it, take a deep breath and look into your own eyes. This is a moment of self-connection.

On your piece of paper, jot down three things you'd like to manifest during this moon phase. Be as detailed as possible, channeling Virgo's precision.

Holding the mirror again, read each intention out loud to your reflection, adding the phrase *"I see it, I believe it, I will achieve it,"* at the end of each intention.

Close your eyes, hold the piece of paper with your intentions, and visualize them coming to fruition. Feel the warmth of the candle's flame representing the warmth and light these intentions will bring to your life.

Once done, express gratitude to the universe and the New Moon in Virgo for providing clarity and focus.

Fold your paper and keep it in a place you visit daily (like beside your bed, on your work desk, or inside your journal). This acts as a constant reminder of the intentions you set.

Virgo is sharp-minded, health-oriented and recognizes what needs to be fixed. She's also a natural boss babe able to do things her own magical way. Efficient and able to achieve all she sets out to achieve, Virgo is a manifesting goddess. Be open to her guidance.

Full Moon in Virgo

Full Moon in Virgo Manifesting Tips

Ah, the Full Moon in Virgo – it's like having a fairy godmother who's also a top-notch organizer. You see, Virgo is all about precision, detail, and practicality. When the moon shines full in this sign, it's not just about dreaming big; it's about laying out the practical steps to make that dream come true. Think of it as the universe handing you a magical planner, where wishes are translated into actionable tasks. With Virgo's meticulous touch, this Full Moon helps in refining your manifestation process, ensuring that every magical intention is backed by a tangible plan. It's like saying, "Dream, but also dot the i's and cross the t's!"

Full Moon in Virgo Ritual

Divine Virgo Vibes Jar

Harness the meticulous energy of Virgo and the nurturing essence of the goddess to craft a manifesting magic jar.

MATERIALS:

- A clear glass jar with a lid (a mason jar works great)
- Earth-toned ribbons or threads
- Small healing stones (like sunstone, amazonite, or rose quartz)

- Fresh earth or potting soil
- Seeds (basil or chamomile work well)
- Paper and pen
- A figure or image of a goddess (a goddess associated with earth or harvest would be ideal)
- Moonlit water (water that's been left under the moonlight for a night)

DIRECTIONS:

Start by placing your jar outside or on a windowsill where it can soak up the Full Moon energy. Let it sit for a few minutes.

On a piece of paper, write down a specific intention you'd like to manifest. Fold it up and place it at the bottom of the jar.

Place the figure or image of your chosen goddess in the jar, asking her to bless your intention.

Pour a layer of fresh earth or potting soil into the jar, symbolizing Virgo's earthy nature and grounding your intentions.

Place a few seeds onto the soil, representing the potential for growth and the realization of your wishes.

Add your chosen healing stones to the jar. These act as little guardians, infusing the jar with positive and manifesting energy.

Pour the moonlit water into the jar until the soil is damp. This water carries the energy of the Full Moon, amplifying your manifesting process.

Tie earth-toned ribbons or threads around the jar, sealing in the energies.

Holding the jar, say: "*Under Virgo's meticulous gaze and the goddess's nurturing ways, I set forth my intentions, ready for brighter days.*"

Place the jar back in the moonlight for the remainder of the night. If possible, let it stay there till the morning, soaking up the dawn's first light.

Over the next month, keep the jar in a place where you'll see it daily, reminding you of your intentions and the magic you've infused.

Here's a brief guide to help the seeds in your jar sprout:

1. Moisture, Not Saturation: Seeds need moisture to sprout, but they don't need to be submerged in water. Make sure the soil is moist to the touch but not waterlogged.

2. Daily Check: Open the jar daily to allow fresh air in. This also gives you the opportunity to check the moisture level of the soil.

3. Little Watering: If the soil feels dry, sprinkle a little water to moisten it. A spray bottle can be handy for this, as it allows you to add moisture without overwatering.

4. Light Matters: Once the seeds sprout, they will need light to grow. Move the jar to a location where it can receive indirect sunlight.

5. Bigger Home: If you notice the sprouts are growing bigger and seem cramped in the jar, it might be time to transfer them to a larger pot or directly to the garden, where they can continue to grow.

Remember, the goal of this ritual jar is more symbolic and magical than agricultural. The seeds represent potential and growth, mirroring your intentions. If they do sprout, it's a beautiful bonus and a tangible sign of your intentions taking root and growing. If they don't, the symbolic act of planting them still holds powerful energy and intention.

Have fun and trust the process, knowing that the Virgo Full Moon and the divine goddess are both by your side!

Moon in Libra

MANIFESTING ENERGIES: Relationships, Balance, and Harmony

New Moon in Libra

New Moon in Libra Manifesting Tips

New Moon in Libra? It's like getting an invite to the universe's most elegant soirée, where all dreams find their perfect dance partners. You see, Libra, with its charm and grace, is all about balance, beauty, and relationships. So, when the moon is new in this sign, it's a golden ticket to manifest not just for yourself but in harmony with others. Think of it as planting seeds in a cosmic garden where everything complements each other. Whether you're wishing for love, a collaboration, or just some peace and balance in life, the New Moon in Libra gives your intentions that extra sprinkle of magic where everything just... aligns. Ready to waltz with the stars?

New Moon in Libra Ritual

Tap into the balanced, relational energy of Libra to bring alignment and connection to your desires.

MATERIALS:

- A small, heart-shaped box or container, or box with a heart drawn on it
- Pen and small pieces of paper
- Two small balance stones (like rose quartz and clear quartz)
- A feather (to symbolize the airy nature of Libra)
- A playlist of soft, harmonious tunes

DIRECTIONS:

Start your chosen playlist. Let the harmonious tunes set the mood, aligning your energies with Libra's grace.

Take a few moments to reflect on what you wish to manifest - things that would bring balance and beauty into your life.

On the pieces of paper, write down these harmonious wishes. Fold them and place them inside your box.

Hold the two balance stones in each hand. Close your eyes and visualize them grounding and harmonizing your desires. Place them in the box with your wishes.

Lay the feather on top, signifying the gentle touch of Libra ensuring your intentions take flight with ease and grace.

Close the box and hold it close to your heart. Whisper, *"Under the gentle glow of the Libra New Moon, may my wishes find balance, connection, and bloom soon."*

Place the heart-shaped box under your pillow or on your nightstand for the night, letting the New Moon energy further charge your intentions as you sleep.

Here's what you can do with your box in the long term:

1. Monthly Review: Every New Moon, revisit the box to see how your intentions are unfolding. You might be surprised to find how many have come to fruition or have evolved.

2. Renew & Refresh: If a particular wish has manifested or no longer serves you, remove it from the box and write down a new intention, adding it back in. This keeps the box's energy fresh and aligned with your evolving desires.

3. Sacred Space: Keep the box in a special place, like an altar, a personal sanctuary, or a dedicated corner in your home. This turns it into a focal point of manifestation energy.

4. Annual Libra New Moon Ritual: Make it an annual tradition! Every year, during the New Moon in Libra, take out the box and review, renew, and recharge your intentions, making it a special occasion to look forward to.

5. Gratitude Ritual: Every once in a while, open the box and express gratitude for the intentions that have come to life. This act of thankfulness amplifies the box's manifesting energy.

Full Moon in Libra

Full Moon in Libra Manifesting Tips

When the Full Moon dances in Libra, it's like the universe sets up the most enchanting cosmic ballroom. Imagine Libra as the graceful host, urging you to find balance, harmony, and beauty in your desires. This moon phase is a golden moment for manifesting relationships, partnerships, or anything that requires equilibrium and connection. It's not just about what you want, but also about how your wishes harmonize with the world around you. Think of it as tuning your manifestation radio to the frequency of love, beauty, and collaboration. With Libra's charm under this moonlit night, you're not just casting your intentions; you're artistically painting them onto the vast canvas of the universe, promising beauty and balance in return.

Full Moon in Libra Ritual

Channel the harmonizing and relational energies of Libra to create balance in your manifesting journey.

MATERIALS:

- Two white or pastel-colored candles (representing balance)
- A small set of scales (or an image of scales)
- Pen and two pieces of paper
- A rose quartz crystal (or any pretty stone or trinket)
- Your favorite calming or harmonious background music

DIRECTIONS:

Play your chosen background music softly, creating a peaceful ambiance.

Place the two candles on either side of your scales, representing the balance Libra seeks. Light them up, and as you do, envision the balanced energy they bring.

Think of a personal desire you wish to manifest and an external desire (something related to relationships or harmony with others).

On one piece of paper, write down the personal desire. On the other, jot down the external one. Place each paper on opposing sides of the scales, visualizing the balance between self and others.

Hold the rose quartz (or chosen trinket) in your hand, feeling its calming and loving energies. Think of it as absorbing the Full Moon in Libra's energy. Then, place it on the scale's center, symbolizing harmony and love connecting your two desires.

As the candles burn, recite aloud or in your heart, *"Under the Libra Full Moon's radiant glow, may balance, beauty, and harmony in my desires flow."*

Once you feel your intentions are set and the energy feels right, blow out the candles, thanking the moon and Libra for their guiding light.

Fold the pieces of paper around the rose quartz or trinket, keeping it in a special place until the next Full Moon. It will serve as a reminder of the balance you're manifesting in your life.

Moon in Scorpio

MANIFESTING ENERGIES: Transformation, Intimacy, and Uncovering Hidden Truths

New Moon in Scorpio

New Moon in Scorpio Manifesting Tips

Dive into a New Moon in Scorpio, and it's like you've unlocked a secret door to a hidden chamber of deep desires and untapped power. Imagine Scorpio as that mysterious friend who whispers, "Let's uncover the truths buried within." This moon is all about plunging into the emotional depths, bringing to light those raw, intense wishes you might've been shy to admit, even to yourself. When setting intentions under this moon, it's not just about surface-level goals; it's about connecting to the core of your desires, where magic is most potent. So, when you manifest under this inky Scorpio moon, it's like sending a powerful ripple into the universe, one that says, "I'm ready for transformative change!"

New Moon in Scorpio Ritual

The Scorpio Treasure Box Manifestation

PURPOSE: Dive deep into the transformative energies of Scorpio to uncover and set your most profound intentions.

MATERIALS:

- A small box (like a jewelry or trinket box)
- Pen and small pieces of paper
- A few gemstones or crystals (black obsidian, malachite, or any you feel drawn to)
- A tealight or small candle (black or deep red to align with Scorpio's energy)

DIRECTIONS:

1. In a dimly lit room, light the tealight or candle. The low light setting channels Scorpio's mysterious and introspective vibe.

2. Sit comfortably and take a few deep breaths. Allow your mind to delve deep, thinking of intentions rooted in your truest desires. Let the transformative Scorpio energy guide you.

3. On the pieces of paper, jot down these deep-seated wishes or goals. Fold them up and place them in the box.

4. Add your chosen crystals or gemstones to the box. They serve to amplify and protect your intentions.

5. Close the box and hold it in your hands. Visualize it filling up with the dark, magnetic energy of the New Moon in Scorpio. Imagine your intentions absorbing this energy, preparing to transform into reality.

6. Place your Scorpio Treasure Box in a special spot, like your bedside table, altar, or sacred space. You can revisit it, adding more intentions or just soaking in its energy during the moon cycle.

Blow out the candle while expressing gratitude to the universe and Scorpio for aiding in this powerful manifesting process. *"As I close this ritual, I honor the deep, transformative energies of Scorpio and the potent potential of the New Moon. I trust that the intentions sealed within this treasure box will unfurl in the universe's perfect timing, guided by the mysteries and magic of Scorpio's embrace. With gratitude and a heart full of hope, I release my desires to the cosmos, knowing they are heard, nurtured, and set on a path of becoming. Until our next dance under the moonlight, blessed be."*

Full Moon in Scorpio

Full Moon in Scorpio Manifesting Tips

Full Moon shining in Scorpio is the universe inviting you to a deep dive into waters shimmering with mystical secrets. Think of Scorpio as that intense, soulful friend who sees right through to your core and challenges you to embrace both your shadows and light. Manifesting under this moon isn't just surface-level stuff; it's about tapping into those deep desires, the ones that stir your soul and might even scare you a bit with their power. Scorpio energy pushes you to go beyond the ordinary and to transform your deepest wishes into reality. So, under this moon, it's not just about what you want, but about understanding the depths of why you want it. It's a magnetic dance of passion, depth, and transformative magic!

Full Moon in Scorpio Ritual

Dive deep into Scorpio's transformative waters to reflect, understand, and manifest your most profound desires.

MATERIALS:

- A mirror (handheld or any size you're comfortable with)
- Crimson, black, or deep purple candle (channeling Scorpio's intense energy)

- A bowl of water (symbolizing Scorpio's water element)
- Pen and paper
- A few rose petals (for added depth and connection to emotions)
- Your favorite calming or mysterious background music

DIRECTIONS:

Fill your bowl with water, then sprinkle in the rose petals. This water will capture the energy of the Full Moon and the essence of Scorpio.

Light your candle and place it beside the bowl. Look into the mirror under the moonlight. As you gaze into your reflection, ask yourself: "What deep desires is my soul yearning to manifest?"

Take your pen and paper, and write down the desires and feelings that surface, no matter how profound or intense they might be. This is Scorpio's energy guiding you to acknowledge what's beneath the surface.

Read your desires aloud to the moon, whispering or speaking passionately, however you feel. Imagine these desires rising with the smoke of the candle, being absorbed by the Full Moon's glow.

Dip your fingers into the bowl of water and lightly sprinkle some onto your face. Feel the rejuvenating energy of the water, symbolizing Scorpio's power of transformation and rebirth.

Let loose and have a little dance to your background music, letting the energies of the Full Moon and Scorpio flow through you. Feel the joy and gratitude for the deep insights you've gained.

As you extinguish the candle, say: *"Under Scorpio's deep gaze and the Full Moon's radiant light, my desires are set free, ready to transform and take flight."*

Pour the water and roses into a glass jar. Place outdoors and charge under the Full Moon. Bring your water in before Sunrise.

Fold your paper and keep it under your pillow for the night. This simple act is like sending a message to the universe, with Scorpio as the messenger.

The next morning, you can either keep the paper by your bed or in a special place.

Here are some ideas what to do with the Moon-Charged Full Moon in Scorpio Water:

1. Moon Bath: Pour the water over your hands or feet, feeling the coolness and the moon's energy cleansing and recharging you.

2. Sacred Space Cleansing: Use the water to cleanse your sacred space, altar, or meditation corner. Sprinkle a few drops around the area to purify and infuse it with the Full Moon's energy.

3. Plant Nourishment: Water your indoor plants with the moon-charged water, channeling the idea of growth and transformation.

4. Crystal Cleanse: If you have crystals, cleanse them with the water. It will refresh their energy, making them even more potent for your spiritual practices.

5. Letter Seal: After writing your intention on the paper, you can dip your fingers in the water and sprinkle or dab a few drops onto the paper, sealing your intention with the Full Moon's energy.

6. Return to Earth: Pour the water back onto the ground or at the base of a tree as an offering, thanking the moon and Scorpio for their guidance. As you do this, visualize your intentions being absorbed by the Earth and being transformed into reality.

Remember, the power of any ritual or activity lies in the intention and the energy you put into it. The actions are symbolic, helping to reinforce and channel those intentions. You've got the power, Beautiful!

Moon in Sagittarius

MANIFESTING ENERGIES: Adventure, Philosophy,
and Seeking Higher Truths

New Moon in Sagittarius

New Moon in Sagittarius Tips for Manifesting

When there's a New Moon in Sagittarius, it's like the universe just handed you a magic-infused compass pointing straight towards your wildest dreams. You know Sagittarius, right? That free-spirited, always-up-for-an-adventure pal?

Well, with the New Moon in this sign, setting intentions becomes a delightful mix of hopeful optimism and boundless exploration. It's less about manifesting things and more about manifesting experiences, journeys, and growth. With Sagittarius guiding this lunar energy, you're not just wishing upon a star; you're aiming your arrow at it, ready to leap and soar. It's a cosmic invitation to dream big and chase even bigger!

New Moon in Sagittarius Ritual

MATERIALS:

- Star-shaped stickers or confetti (easily found at craft stores)
- A piece of paper (preferably dark blue or black to resemble the night sky) I used dark wrapping paper
- A silver or gold pen
- A small pot or container
- A little bit of sand or dirt
- A small candle (adventure-inspired scent, like pine or cedar, is a bonus)

DIRECTIONS:

Spread out your piece of paper on a flat surface, representing the vast universe.

Taking a moment to feel the energy of the New Moon and Sagittarius, write down what you hope to manifest on the back of your star-shaped stickers or on the confetti pieces using the silver or gold pen.

Stick or place your written stars on the paper. Imagine each star as a wish or goal, shining brightly in the universe.

Place the small pot or container on the paper and fill it with a bit of sand or dirt. Plant the candle in the center and light it. This represents the fiery and guiding arrow of Sagittarius, illuminating your intentions.

As the candle burns, close your eyes and visualize your intentions shooting like arrows or stars into the universe, knowing that they're on their way to manifesting.

Embody the joyful and free-spirited energy of Sagittarius by dancing around your candlelit "universe." Let loose and have fun!

Once you've finished dancing, blow out the candle and say, *"By the adventurous spirit of Sagittarius and the power of the New Moon, my dreams are now set in motion, ready to shoot forth and become my reality."*

Fold or roll up your paper universe and place it somewhere special, like near your bed or in your sacred space. Every time you see it, remember the intentions you set and the cosmic dance you shared with Sagittarius.

Let the New Moon's energy guide you and enjoy the journey!

Full Moon in Sagittarius

Full Moon in Sagittarius Tips for Manifesting

When there's a Full Moon in Sagittarius, it's like the universe is handing out enchanted arrows for our quivers. Imagine Sagittarius as that adventurous, optimistic friend who urges you to shoot for the stars and dream big. Under this Full Moon, aspirations get supercharged with a spirit of adventure, optimism, and a thirst for knowledge. It's the perfect time to manifest not just tangible things, but also experiences and personal growth. This moon says, "Why just wish for it when you can aim high and chase after it?" So, with the Sagittarian moonlight as your guide, your manifesting powers become a thrilling quest filled with possibilities.

Full Moon in Sagittarius Ritual

Time to embrace the bold and adventurous energy of Sagittarius to manifest dreams with an optimistic spirit. Woohoo!

MATERIALS:

- A small notebook or pieces of paper

- A pen or marker

- A bow (it can be a toy bow or even a crafted one from a stick and string, or you can do what I do and make a pretend one)

- A few "arrows" (you can use craft sticks or even rolled-up paper)
- A flashlight, torch, or lantern

DIRECTIONS:

Find a cozy spot indoors or outdoors. Turn on some uplifting music, perhaps with a beat that gets your heart pumping.

In your notebook or on your paper pieces, jot down 3 big dreams or goals. Let your imagination run wild and free, just as a Sagittarius would!

Write one dream or goal on each of your craft stick or paper "arrows". These arrows symbolize the Sagittarian energy of aiming for what you desire.

As night falls and the Full Moon shines bright, head outside with your bow, arrows, and flashlight, torch, or lantern. The aim is to find a quiet, open space where you can "shoot" your arrows.

With each dream arrow, take a moment to focus on your goal. Then facing east, "shoot" your arrow into the distance (if using a toy bow) or place it on the ground pointing towards the moon, shooting imaginary arrows with your "pretend" bow, symbolizing your intent to send your dream into the universe.

With all your arrows aimed and your intentions set, celebrate with a little dance under the moonlight. Feel the joy, optimism, and adventurous spirit of Sagittarius filling you up! Yeee-haw!

Once you're done, gather your arrows, sit down, and shine your light onto your goals. Spend a few moments visualizing the journey towards achieving them.

After your moonlit quest, find a special place in your home for your arrows—a spot where you'll see them regularly. It could be on a windowsill, a dedicated sacred space, or even taped to your bathroom mirror. These arrows will serve as daily reminders of the goals you've set. Every time you see them, take a moment to visualize your aim and reignite the adventurous spirit of Sagittarius.

This ritual brings out the playful, adventurous nature of Sagittarius, making manifesting both fun and meaningful. Enjoy your moonlit manifesting adventure under the Sagittarius Full Moon!

Moon in Capricorn

MANIFESTING ENERGIES: Ambition, Career, and Structures

New Moon in Capricorn

New Moon in Capricorn Manifesting Tips

There's something so potent about a New Moon in Capricorn when setting intentions. Capricorn is that friend who's always got a blueprint for their dreams and is ready to start from the ground up. With the New Moon in this sign, it's like being handed a cosmic toolkit for building dreams brick by brick. It nudges you to plant seeds of ambition and lay down practical steps to reach your goals. A New Moon in Capricorn isn't just about dreaming; it's about rolling up your sleeves and getting ready to work with the universe to craft your future. If ever there was a time to chart out your goals and start fresh with clear direction, this is it!

Remember, Capricorn is represented by the goat which is the symbol of abundance, fertility, and good luck. What new seeds do you want to plant in this fertile cosmic soil, because Capricorn is going to lend her energy and confidence to accomplish it.

New Moon in Capricorn Ritual

This activity illuminates your path towards your professional aspirations and helps you embody the determination and resilience of Capricorn's mountain goat.

MATERIALS:

- A dark blue or black candle
- A carving tool
- Essential oils like vetiver or patchouli
- Comfortable seating
- Calming background music (optional, mountain or nature-themed would be ideal)

DIRECTIONS:

Choose a quiet place where you won't be disturbed. If you're using background music, begin it now, allowing the serene sounds to envelop the space.

Take the dark blue or black candle and use the carving tool to inscribe symbols or words that represent your career goals. Think of these inscriptions as your roadmap to the peak of your mountain. Anoint the candle with your chosen essential oils, infusing it with your intentions. (If you don't have any oils, hold in between your hands and imbue the manifesting energies into your candle.)

As you light the candle, focus on its flame. Let its light represent the guidance and clarity you seek on your career path.

Sit comfortably in front of the burning candle. Close your eyes and take several deep breaths, centering yourself. Visualize a vast mountain landscape bathed in the soft glow of the candle's light. This mountain represents the journey of your career and the aspirations you aim to achieve.

Picture yourself as the determined mountain goat of Capricorn. Start your ascent, feeling the weight and importance of each step. As you climb, visualize the challenges you might face in your career. Visualize yourself overcoming each obstacle you encounter, recognizing each has made you stronger and more determined. With the flame of the candle guiding you, let its light shine on paths and opportunities you hadn't seen before.

After a determined climb, visualize yourself reaching the mountain's peak. From here, take in the view. It is breathtaking. This peak symbolizes the culmination of your career goals, the milestones you wish to achieve, and the success you're working towards. Take a moment to bask in the feeling of achievement, letting it inspire and motivate you.

With the vision of the peak fresh in your mind and the candle's light still guiding you, recite an affirmation to solidify your intentions, such as: *"With the determination of the mountain goat and the guidance of the flame, I ascend to my highest potential."*

When you feel ready, bring your focus back to the room. Take a few deep cleansing breaths, feeling the renewed energy and purpose from your meditation anchor within your soul. Express gratitude to the energies you've worked with — the steadfast mountain goat, the illuminating candle, and the grounding Capricorn energy.

You can choose to let the candle burn out on its own or snuff it out, saving it for the future rituals. If you choose the latter, every time you relight it, you'll be rekindling the intentions and energies from this ritual.

Every time you come across a mountain goat in advertisements or randomly, know your dreams are being supported and encouraged!

By blending the candle ritual with the mountain meditation, you create a powerful synergy that not only helps clarify and illuminate your career ambitions but also strengthens your resolve and determination to achieve them. Remember to revisit this ritual during future New Moons in Capricorn or whenever you need to rekindle your professional focus.

Full Moon in Capricorn

Full Moon in Capricorn Manifesting Tips

You know, there's something uniquely grounding about a Full Moon in Capricorn when it comes to manifesting. Imagine Capricorn as that super-organized friend who always has a plan and a checklist. With the Full Moon's glow in this sign, it's like our ambitions and practical side merge with a touch of lunar magic. It's the ideal time to get really clear about your goals and make them happen. The Full Moon in Capricorn is like a celestial board meeting where dreams are pitched, plans are laid out, and the universe nods in agreement, saying, "Let's make this real." So, if you've been waiting for the right moment to turn those big dreams into tangible realities, this moon's energy is your cosmic green light!

Full Moon in Capricorn Ritual

This ritual celebrates the grounding Capricorn energy, turning big dreams into bite-sized, achievable steps, all while having fun.

MATERIALS:

- A few pebbles or small stones
- Permanent markers of various colors
- A paper and pen
- A potted plant or your garden patch
- Some fun background music (perhaps some earthy or motivational tunes)

DIRECTIONS:

Setting the Mood: Begin by playing some music. The background tunes should help you feel relaxed and joyful. Dancing a little bit to shake off any tension is highly encouraged!

Dream Big: On your paper, jot down a big goal or dream you have. Don't overthink it—just let your heart speak.

Break It Down: Think of three small steps or actions that'll help you reach that goal. These are like your "mini-goals".

Rock Your Goals: Take your pebbles or stones. Using the markers, write each of your three mini-goals on a separate stone. These stones represent the grounded, steadfast energy of Capricorn.

Plant the Dream: Dig a small hole in your potted plant or garden patch. Place your paper with the big goal written on it into the hole. As you cover it with soil, imagine you're planting your dream, ready for it to grow.

Garden of Intentions: Place your three "goal rocks" around the spot where you planted your dream. These rocks act as markers and reminders of the small steps you'll take towards your big goal.

Celebrate: With your dream planted and your steps laid out, take a moment to dance, sing, or simply bask under the Full Moon's glow. Feel grateful for the journey ahead and trust that your intentions are set.

Have regular check-ins. Every time you water your plant or spend time in your garden, let the goal rocks remind you of your intentions. Remember to celebrate each small step you take and know that with each one, you're closer to your big dream.

Moon in Aquarius

MANIFESTING ENERGIES: Community, Innovation, and Humanitarian Pursuits

New Moon in Aquarius

New Moon in Aquarius Manifesting Tips

New Moon in Aquarius! That's like getting a cosmic nudge to think outside the box and sprinkle a bit of stardust on your wildest dreams. Picture Aquarius as that quirky, visionary friend who always encourages you to see beyond the norm and reach for the unconventional.

With the New Moon in this sign, it's the perfect time to manifest dreams that might seem a tad eccentric or futuristic to others. Aquarius whispers, *"Why fit in when you were born to stand out?"* So, when you're setting your intentions under this moon, don't be afraid to break some molds and dream of the world not as it is, but as it could be. It's all about innovation, idealism, and that dash of magic only Aquarius can bring!

Aquarius is the Rebel of the Zodiac so use this prime opportunity to manifest that crazy, wild, what-you've-always-wanted-but-been-afraid-to-ask-dream!

New Moon in Aquarius Ritual

MATERIALS:

- A shimmering blue or silver candle, echoing the astral colors of Aquarius
- An aquamarine or clear quartz crystal, vessels for ethereal visions
- A bowl of moonlit water (collect rainwater or natural water under the New Moon's glow if possible, otherwise use distilled water or boil tap water for one minute before using)
- Paper and a silver ink pen
- Star-shaped confetti or glitters
- Incense, preferably star anise or frankincense to bridge earthly intentions with celestial realms

DIRECTIONS:

Prepare a space where you won't be disturbed. Place your items. Get comfortable.

As you light your incense, visualize starlight threads connecting you to galaxies near and far, grounding you in cosmic wisdom. Take a cleansing breath and allow yourself to align with this stellar energy.

When ready, whisper to the flames, *"May the forward-thinking spirit of Aquarius illuminate my path to manifestation."*

Peer into your bowl of moonlit water, letting the Aquarian energies wash over you. Imagine the Aquarian Water Bearer pouring from her jug, sharing ideas and dreams, allowing your own aspirations to ripple and swirl within the water.

With your silver pen, on your paper, script your most profound dreams and aspirations. Think of what innovations or freedoms you wish to manifest. Be bold, be visionary! Be very Starchild!

When finished, sprinkle the star confetti or glitter over your written dreams. Imagine each sparkle as a beacon in the cosmos, magnetizing your manifestations.

Next, hold your chosen crystal above the bowl, letting it absorb the moonlit reflections. Whisper your dreams to the crystal, letting it become a talisman of your Aquarian aspirations.

Raising your arms skyward, recite: *"By the boundless stars and the visionary spirit of Aquarius, may my dreams weave into the cosmic tapestry, manifesting for the greater good and my soul's journey. With harm to none and blessings to all."*

Thank the constellations, the mysterious waters, and the universe for their guidance, whispering, *"As the cosmos expands, so too shall my visions take form. So mote it be."*

Gently extinguish your candle. Pour the water in a glass jar and keep until the next new moon. You can set this out under the next Full Moon and charge the water with additional manifesting energies. At the next New Moon, pour the water into the earth or someplace outdoors in a location that feels special to you, saying,

> *"As I return this moonlit essence to the Earth,*
> *May its radiant energy bless the ground it touches.*
> *Moon above, Earth below,*
> *Let this water's flow bring growth, healing, and harmony.*
> *I offer gratitude for the cycles and the tides,*
> *May this blessing ripple far and wide.*
> *So mote it be."*

Keep the charged crystal and your scripted dreams near your sleeping space. Each night, before drifting to dreams, hold the crystal and visualize one of your intentions coming to fruition.

The Aquarian New Moon is a portal to otherworldly visions and altruistic dreams. By aligning your manifestation energies with this cosmic doorway, you beckon forth magic that has the power to transform not just individual lives, but the very fabric of the universe. Claim your power you beautiful star traveler!

Full Moon in Aquarius

Full Moon in Aquarius Manifesting Tips

Aquarius brings the out-of-the-box thinking. What is being revealed? Is there an area you'd like clarification? What have been all your successes? This is time for a major celebration! This sets yourself up energetically for a big manifesting win!

Aquarius will share her opinions and guidance under this Full Moon to ensure you're on the right track. Anything left to question, needed shifts, or adjustments, this air sign will provide insight. She'll most likely pour out unconventional ways to attract, release, and celebrate. Be open during this Full Moon as insight doesn't just trickle, it flows. Be poised to take action. You'll have much to celebrate by September.

Full Moon in Aquarius Ritual

This is a wonderful time to engage in a full moon ritual with others. If there isn't a group setting you feel comfortable or desire to join, create your own by inviting Goddess Sopdet, Goddess Isis and Goddess Sekhmet.

Go outdoors with supplies for writing and drawing, your favorite crystals and a glass of water.

Set your intention for the crystals and water to be charged and imbued with the energy of this ritual.

Gaze at the moon allowing yourself to fill with appreciation for its beauty and power. Visualize yourself standing at the edge on a circle. Invite the goddesses to join by saying,

> "Goddess Sopdet, goddess of the brightest star and bringer of the new year, please honor me with your presence in this circle.
>
> Goddess Isis, queen of the throne and goddess of healing and magic, please honor me with your presence in this circle.
>
> Goddess Sekhmet, she who is powerful and goddess of the sun, please honor me with your presence in this circle."

When you sense they've joined, imagine reaching out and holding each other's hands. The circle naturally forming with this action. Imagine making contact with each of the goddesses. Your circle is safe and set.

In a clear and loud voice announce, "I thank the goddesses for their wisdom and their presence. I thank the moon goddess for her light. I recognize and thank my own goddess within and I open and accept all the messages of clarity and love on this special night."

Raise your hands above your head to the moon. While still holding the goddesses hands begin singing "hum" pronounced, "hoom." Raise your voice while chanting "hoom." When you feel the vibration of the chant flowing through your body, release your hands and wave to the moon. Dance, cheer, smile and laugh. Bring your hands to your heart in a prayer form and say, "It is so." Bow to each goddess while thanking them and releasing them.

Immediately journal or doodle. Let all the guidance flow. Sip on the water while writing or save as special moon water. Journal for the next seven days.

Keep your journal and crystals near your bed or in your sacred space.

This Full Moon in Aquarius has washed away the old and is powerfully welcoming in the fulfillment of the new!

Moon in Pisces

MANIFESTING ENERGIES: Intuition, Dreams, and Spiritual Connections.

New Moon in Pisces

New Moon in Pisces Manifesting Tips

When there's a New Moon in Pisces, it's like the universe is giving a fresh start with a touch of magic. Think of Pisces as that dreamy friend who encourages you to listen to your heart and imagination. So, when you're setting goals or thinking about what you want during this time, it's like having a little extra inspiration in the air. It's the perfect moment to dream big, feel deeply, and let yourself believe in the possibilities.

Pisces brings her gifts of intuition, sensitivity, creativity, and compassion. You'll be able to go for what you truly desire and know that you are worthy of this. Implement elements of art into your New Moon intentions. For example, journal your New Moon desires and then add doodles and splashes of color around it. Sprinkle with confetti. Add stickers. Have fun and trust your intuition as you guide the manifesting energies.

New Moon in Pisces Ritual

Get in a quiet and safe place free from distractions as you'll be doing a mini-meditation, followed by an art activity. Include your chosen form of art such as: canvas and paints, watercolors and paper, pen and paper, journal and pen, or magazine cut-outs and paper.

Take a cleansing breath, relaxing into your seat. Closing your eyes, direct your mind, emotions, and soul in a state of gratitude. Focus on something you're truly grateful for. When you feel an energetic shift, send love and appreciation from your heart chakra. Bring your hands to your heart. Take a cleansing breath and smile.

When you feel ready, imagine your new seed/desire/new moon intention having manifested. Take a moment to connect as if you have time traveled and are present in the manifested time. Observe all through your senses making notes of everything you notice. Linger here. Enjoy this excursion to your successful future. And when you feel ready to leave, ask your senses for one final check.

Open your eyes and begin painting, drawing, or doodling on your paper. Draw or even write anything that intuitively is shown to you. Stay in the flow. Pisces will help. While creating your art, continue to daydream in the space that your new moon intentions have manifested. When you feel complete take a cleansing breath. There isn't a set time. Feel free to set a timer if you're a perfectionist and need to create a hard stop! Most of all, enjoy this process and let the magic flow!

When finished, place this art in your sacred space, saying, *"Thank you for this manifested blessing. I accept and receive this or something better."*

Create an affirmation for your intention. State daily as you visit and view your art. You may place crystals or aromatherapy by your art to boost your manifesting energies.

On the sixth day, light a yellow birthday candle by your art. Say, *"Thank you for the clear path to this manifested blessing. With my breath, I release the path to the Divine."* Blow out the candle, knowing your air and breath is breathing new energies into your dreams. Leave the candle by your art.

New Moon in Pisces will heighten your intuition. Work with this moon cycle as new ideas and paths to manifest will also be revealed!

Full Moon in Pisces

Full Moon in Pisces Manifesting Tips

When there's a Full Moon in Pisces, it feels like everything's got this soft, magical glow to it.

The air is thick with magic and emotions. Think of Pisces as that intuitive friend who always knows what they're feeling and what they want deep down. So, under this Full Moon, our ability to tap into our own emotions and desires becomes supercharged. It's the perfect time to really dive deep into what we truly want and manifest those dreams into reality. When we're in tune with our feelings, as Pisces often is, our manifestations become more potent and aligned with our true selves. Manifesting under this moon isn't just about asking for what you want—it's about feeling it, believing in it, and letting the universe know you accept you're worth it.

Full Moon in Pisces Ritual

This would be a great time to soak in the tub, relax in the shower or sit under the Full Moon sky and bathe in the light and loving energy. Ask for any insight, subtle shifts needed or anything needing changed so your New Moon intentions can be manifested easier. Pisces may communicate through a song, piece of art or subtly through your ESP, extra sensory perception. This will be a time for being hyper observant and noticing any intuitive messages.

To ensure you tap into this unique and powerful manifesting energy, practice morning and evening insight for the three days prior, day of the full moon and three days after.

In the morning: spend seventy seconds or more visualizing your new moon intentions have manifested. Placing your hands over your heart, feel the joy and gratitude with this manifested. Take a cleansing breath .and gently move your hands in tiny circles as if massaging this blessing into your heart. When you feel complete, take a cleansing breath and give yourself a hug. Journal any insight that your received.

In the evening: ask angels for guidance in your dreams. Ask for clarity, anything you need to release, any actions to take, or even just loving messages of inspiration and encouragement. Ask angels to help you remember your dreams. Before you take any movement out of bed, immediately upon waking, journal any feelings, memories, or impressions from your dreams. Add any words, symbols, or insight.

This Pisces Full Moon is sensitive to your needs, so don't be surprised if she subtly suggests working with spirit guides during this time. They want to help make your dreams come true! If you knew your fairy godmother could truly deliver, what would you ask for? That's this energy flowing right now!

Every cosmic event, every zodiac shift, every moon phase is an invitation. An invitation to manifest, to dream, and to co-create. Hold your intentions close, let the cosmos be your guide, and watch as the universe conspires in your favor. Here's to endless possibilities and a future where dreams aren't just dreamt—they're manifested!

★

ABOUT THE AUTHOR

Manifesting expert and lifetime psychic, Trish Mckinnley, helps your dreams become a reality. With clients around the world, Creator of Goddessology® and Soul & Spirit Magazine's very first Rising Star, Trish brings fun, normalcy and understanding to the "woowoo."

Having manifested her happily-ever-after – complete with modern-day castle and handsome prince (and this was after everyone told her it'd be impossible as a single mom with six kids) – Trish shares her unique and easy-to-implement methods and secrets to unleashing your inner manifesting magic and living the life of your dreams!

And when she's not helping you gain the life you desire, she can be found running around the farm with another cup of coffee, snacking on candy, and rescuing animals.

VISIT HER AT
WWW.SHINEANDALIGNWITHTRISH.COM

Made in the USA
Middletown, DE
08 March 2024

50473251R00195